I Loved a Girl

I Loved a Girl
Love Is a Feeling to Be Learned
Living with Unfulfilled Desires
My Beautiful Feeling
My Parents Are Impossible
My Wife Made Me a Polygamist
A Baby Just Now?
All a Man Can Be
Love Yourself
Spiritual Dryness
Martin Luther's Quiet Time

I LOVED A GIRL

(including I LOVED A YOUNG MAN)

*A Private Correspondence between Two
Young Africans and Their Pastor*

Compiled by

WALTER TROBISCH

Foreword by

Josh McDowell

Introduction by

David R. Mace

HarperSanFrancisco

A Division of HarperCollinsPublishers

Library of Congress Cataloging-in-Publication Data

Trobisch, Walter, comp.
   I loved a girl (including I loved [i.e. love] a young man)

   Translation of J'ai aimé une fille and J'aime un jeune homme.
   Reprint of the 1965 ed., which was issued as no. CB12 of Harper chapelbooks.
   1. Family life education. 2. Pastoral counseling. I. Trobisch, Walter, comp. J'aime un jeune homme. English. 1980. II. Title.
HQ10.T713   1980   306.7   88-45681
ISBN 0-06-068454-2

95   RRD   10   9   8   7   6   5

Foreword

I Loved a Girl is a Christian classic. This timeless book has not only been a tremendous help to me personally, but has helped so many others over the years experience more fully the friendship of Jesus Christ and the riches of Christian life and marriage. Published originally in French in 1962 while Walter Trobisch was a missionary in Cameroun, West Africa, this little book has established itself as a classic of Christian teaching. It continues to speak directly to the confusing and discouraging issues so many people— particularly young people—confront today and to set forth the answers Christianity offers.

The letters gathered in *I Loved a Girl* unfold the story of François and Cecile, young Africans caught up in a rapidly changing society, who struggle with the demands of their own emotions and emerging sexuality, and sometimes waver in their commitment to their Christian faith. But if the setting is exotic, the issues faced by these young people and those who act as their spiritual counselors are universal.

In a very concrete way, *I Loved a Girl* holds up a "distant mirror" to our own situation today: their sometimes challenging questions about love, sex, marriage, self-worth, prayer, forgiveness, and fellowship with Christ are the same sort of questions I hear over and over. And the answers that they find—whether through the counsel of their wise and compassionate "Dear Pastor" or from recognizing God's truth in their hearts—offer guidance, encouragement, and hope to all readers.

The story of Cecile and François is set in the context of a rapidly changing society in which old ways and new ideas are in collision. In our lives we don't have to look any further than this morning's headline or tonight's newscast to realize just how unsettled our own society is. Our society seems bent on breaking down traditional value systems—and this is seen as a "good thing" because it gives people the freedom to discover and build their own value systems and become all that they are meant to be.

Sadly, rather than finding themselves set free to realize their full potential, more and more people today are feeling rudderless—adrift in a confusing world without the anchors of personal value and significance. Young people in particular are apt to feel alone and confused; bombarded by conflicting messages from society and their own bodies and emotions; terrified by violence; tempted by drugs, immorality, and materialistic values; and isolated as cogs in a vast machine.

As I've written elsewhere, "People still need to know that they are loved and have worth. Rather than being outdated, this is where Christianity speaks to modern people's needs in a unique way. A personal relationship with Jesus Christ sets and individual free to be all that he or she was created to be." Our belief in our own self-worth is intimately connected with our feelings that we are worthy of being loved.

Love is the heart of *I Loved a Girl*: the love that exists in the fellowship of Christ and that is reflected in the love that exists between a man and woman in Christian marriage. In such a relationship, so beautifully presented by the author, lies the reaffirmation of our value as a person. Walter Trobisch writes, "The most important decision of your life is the decision to follow Christ. The second most important decision is your choice of a marriage partner."

François, over the span of time encompassed by these letters, learns that what he once called "love" was only desire and sexual gratification. Gradually, he comes to understand the true meaning of love in his deepening relationship with Cecile. As his awareness grows, we are reminded that sex is a gift from God and that it finds its proper expression and fulfillment in marriage when husband and wife become "one flesh."

I Loved a Girl confronts frankly many difficult questions about control of sexual desire, fears about sexuality, peer pressure, "experimentation," definitions of manhood and womanhood, promiscuity, infertility, and maturity. From these concerns, the discussion expands to examine issues of guilt and forgiveness, the meaning of grace, the power of prayer, and what it means to live fully the Christian life. At every point in the exchange, Trobisch avoids what he calls "cheap cut-and-dried answers." As a result, his answers are biblically sound, carefully reasoned, informed by medical and psychological facts—and deeply satisfying.

"A Christian is one who can wait," Trobisch reminds an impatient François, "by not waiting you will gain nothing and you will lose much." What would be lost is "freedom, joy, and beauty" that exist only in marriage. And in the sin would come the greatest loss of all: estrangement from Christ, "the perfect example of God's 'perfect love.'"

The witness to so much that is central to the Christian message has brought me again and again to *I Loved a Girl*. The wise and heartfelt counsel it offers is timeless as are the questions it addresses. The choices faced by François and Cecile are the same choices that must be made everyday by thousands of young people everywhere.

Early in *I Loved a Girl,* Walter Trobisch writes to François, "My heart goes out to the many young people today who suffer inwardly, because they must live alone with their problems. If only they could be encouraged to open their hearts to someone who could counsel them!" François responds, "I write to you with growing joy, because I feel that I am no longer left alone, and that gives me new courage." Many who have read this book have found the experience like having a heart-to-heart talk with its author, and have shared something of François' joy as a result.

Through their exchange of letters, François was guided ever deeper into joyful fellowship with Christ. Through the medium of this book, untold readers have made the same journey. It points the way toward the fullness of the promise, while encouraging us, even when our way seems impassable, "Don't lose courage. God is with us, even in the darkness. True faith begins there, where one doesn't see at all. When all else forsakes us, all human hope, all possibility of a solution, then there is only one thing left for us to do: to let ourselves fall into God's arms. God is never closer to us than in such moments. 'Fear not, *only* believe,' the Bible commands. We are only fully in God's hands when we have Him alone."

JOSH D. MCDOWELL

Julian, California
August 1988

Preface
to the 1965 edition

Those who may be shocked by the frankness and intimacy of these letters should know that those who wrote them did not at the time entertain any thought of their communications being published. Later, both the boy, François, and the girl, Cecile, proposed that this correspondence be put into a book because of their belief that the counsel which had helped them might also prove helpful to others.

The book made its first appearance in Africa in 1962. Since that time it has been translated into more than thirty African dialects and a number of European languages. The warm response to date would seem to indicate that François and Cecile were right.

The possibility of book publication in the United States occurred only after François' story, serialized in *His,* a student magazine, produced a vast and unexpected response.

To me and my wife this was inspiring evidence that the human heart is everywhere the same, whether it beats under a black skin or a white one.

WALTER TROBISCH

*Lichtenberg 6
A-4880 St. Georgen i.A.
Austria*

Introduction
to the 1965 edition

BY DAVID R. MACE
EXECUTIVE DIRECTOR
American Association of Marriage Counselors, Inc.

It was in 1962 that Walter Trobisch first sent me a copy of his little book *J'ai Aimé Une Fille. . . .* At that time I had not yet met him, but we had corresponded. I knew that as a missionary in Cameroun, West Africa, he had been especially concerned with the sexual and marital problems of the people among whom he worked. He explained that his little book concerned the personal problems of a young African man who had sought his help; that pastors often had to deal with such problems; and that by publishing the letters he and François had exchanged he hoped it would be possible to help other young people in similar situations.

As I read through these letters I became aware that Walter Trobisch was an unusually sensitive and perceptive man who cared deeply for the people to whom he ministered; and that because of this, he was ready to reach out to these people at the level of their most intimate personal needs in a way few missionaries ever can. I realized also that in the telling of this poignant personal story through the medium of the letters exchanged he had hit upon a powerful dramatic medium for portraying the dilemmas

faced by the young African of today, caught as he is between the backward pull of tribal tradition and the forward pressure of cultural change. As Cecile put it, "the
new and the old bump against each other so suddenly."

It was soon clear that the story of François had an appeal
that extended far beyond Africa. Published at first for the
French-speaking Africans of the Cameroun, the story
soon appeared in German and in English, and was widely
read in Europe. People who would never have thought of
studying African tribal life and customs identified with
this young man's struggles and aspirations, with the way in
which the book portrays the African's hopes and fears as
he emerges from his sheltered past into the maddening
complexity of life in the atomic age. Suddenly the distant,
remote, inscrutable African became for them a very un-
derstandable human being, and his frustrations and indig-
nations found an echo in their own hearts.

At this point the drama of François took a new turn.
Readers who had made his cause their own clamored for
the continuation of his story. The tragic situation in which
we leave François in *I Loved a Girl* . . . is heartrending. His
last words are: "It makes me suffer more than I can bear,
and it will kill me. . . . I do not expect an answer, for there
is none."

What happened next? Obviously, the story had to be
continued. In 1964 the adventures of François were re-
sumed in *I Love a Young Man*. For the first time we were
able to meet Cecile and hear, through the correspondence
with François and with the pastor and his wife, her side of
the story. This took us further still into the complications
young Africans face as the old tribal patterns dissolve before the impact of the modern world.

The appeal of the story now entered a third phase. Originally it had drawn the interest of African youth because

they too were struggling with the problems that plagued François and Cecile. Then it had provided a revealing window through which sympathetic non-Africans could look in upon the complexities of life in the new Africa. And now Western youth discovered that this African couple struggling with the frustrations of their love were not so distant after all. Many of the problems faced by François and Cecile were very similar to their own. They recognized in the experiences of these two the joys and sorrows, triumphs and disasters that inevitably follow when "boy meets girl" the world over. Christian youth especially were able to recognize, under a sultry African sky, the familiar pattern of their own victories and their own defeats.

As the influence of François and Cecile increased, the responsibilities of Walter Trobisch rapidly expanded. Having returned to his native Germany for a secluded period of graduate study, he suddenly found himself inundated by hundreds of letters. From all over Africa, and from the Western world, too, perplexed young people wrote to the sympathetic pastor for guidance.

The friendship of Walter Trobisch and I had established by mail was deepened by a face-to-face encounter when he and his wife Ingrid visited my wife and myself during one of their trips to the United States. The Trobisches are, as one would expect, remarkable people. They speak English, French and German with flawless fluency, and doubtless possess some mastery over African languages as well. Their warm sincerity and the radiance of their Christian faith are contagious, and they share a sensitivity to human needs which derives from their dynamic religious faith. Walter is not the only author in the family. Born in Africa of American parents, Ingrid has told in her charming book *On Our Way Rejoicing* the fascinating story of the pioneer missionary family to which she belongs.

When the American edition of the story of François and Cecile was first projected, Walter asked me to write an Introduction. I count it an honor to do so, for my expectation is that the book will arouse wide interest in this country, as it has already done throughout Africa and Europe.

American readers will have the advantage of reading the full story in one volume. They will find it to be deeply moving, poignantly direct, told with lyrical simplicity. It has the appeal that the love story has had since the dawn of human history. But beneath that level are significant undertones that make it an allegory of the age-old struggle of the soul for purity, integrity, for the Vision of God in a dark, confusing world of seeming injustice and unmeaning.

The drama centers around the traditional African custom of the "bride-price." To a Westerner this seems more barbaric than it actually was, for like many practices of primitive peoples it makes good sense within its cultural framework. The "bride-price" is, for all practical purposes, identical with the *mohar* of the early Hebrews, familiar to us in several of the Old Testament stories.

As Pastor Amos points out, the "bride-price" used to be paid in cattle. When a young man desired to marry a girl, the cattle were transferred from his family to that of the girl, to make up to them for the loss of their daughter. The term "compensation-gift" would more accurately describe this transaction. Significantly, the cattle were not to be disposed of by the girl's family but, for a time at least, to be held in trust. If the girl turned out to be an unsatisfactory wife, the tribal leaders could stipulate that she be returned to her family, and the cattle to the young man's family. In the event that the husband mistreated his wife, however, the tribal leaders might decree that the family could reclaim their daughter and still keep the cattle, thus punishing the badly-behaving husband.

As Africans have adopted a money economy, this sensible system of safeguards has broken down sadly. In recent years, avaricious fathers have been known to sell their daughters to the highest bidders, regardless of the personal implications for the girls. Cecile's father is not a man of this sort. But he needs money badly, and the wealthy Monsieur Henri has position and prestige which, perhaps not only in African eyes, seem to offer Cecile excellent prospects of economic security; whereas the penniless François offers nothing but his love. And, as Pastor Amos plaintively reports: "Cecile's father does not understand what love is. How shall I explain that to him?" Cecile's letter to her father, which closes the book, sums up the entire problem as the daughter tries to justify to her father this completely new approach to marriage which challenges traditional practical considerations.

Other traditional African practices conflict with those of the modern world. The over-riding necessity that a man beget children, and especially sons, was the primary justification for polygamy. Indeed, polygamy was an obligation under the levirate system, which required a man to marry his brother's widow. François is the unhappy child of such an arrangement. And Cecile, in her letter to Ingrid, opens her heart and speaks of fears that every African girl has entertained: "I'm afraid that François will divorce me if I am barren. Or that he will take a second wife."

This obligation to have children challenges, too, the Christian concept of sexual morality that these two young people are trying to accept. Before Cecile there is the temptation to test her fertility before marriage. François is prey to the widespread African belief that a man must prove his manhood by using his sexual powers and especially by fathering a child—and that to restrain sex, withholding his seed, is to risk illness. Goaded by his African friends, again and again he challenges the pastor to justify the exacting demands of the Christian ethic. Western Christian youth will readily identify with him here, for though in the West the arguments are somewhat different, the predicament is the same.

The pastor's difficult task is to justify the Christian ideal of love between man and woman in a cynical world that constantly taints and degrades and exploits. Is the long, hard struggle for integrity and idealism really possible, and is it worthwhile? This is the question that the Christian is continually having to ask himself—in Africa, in Europe, in America. And it is a question that merely happens at the present time to find its focus in the area of sexual behavior. It applies equally to every aspect of the life of man where the way of Christ challenges the convenient compromises that human nature has made with primitive impulse and practical convenience. How much personal struggle and sacrifice can we be expected to undergo in quest of such lofty ideals as integrity, love, unselfishness and justice?

This question raises in turn some very practical dilemmas in the area of church discipline. The story of François sounds a challenge not only to the churches in Africa, but also to those of the Caribbean and elsewhere. Is it justifiable to impose stern discipline, including exclusion from Holy Communion, upon those guilty of sexual misdemeanors, and to be relatively indifferent to the more subtle forms of sin? How can the Church reconcile its functions of representing both a punishing and a forgiving God? If punishment is given considerable emphasis, as in some African churches, does forgiveness become too dear to be meaningful? If there is little or no emphasis on punishment, as in some American churches, does forgiveness become too cheap?

With all these questions, and with others, Pastor Trobisch manfully grapples, as the story of François and Cecile unfolds and the drama of their love is played out against the kaleidoscopic background of African cultural change. We move with them through the gamut of their widely alternating moods—gratitude and anger, faith and doubt, hope and despair. Above the stage, on one side, hovers the dark, demonic figure of Monsieur Henri; on the other that of the pastor, like a guardian angel. The stage is life itself, and the powers are good and evil. It is the eternal drama that is being played out; and the players are not just an African boy and girl, but the human race, whose representatives could just as well be any of us.

March, 1965
Madison, New Jersey

I Loved a Girl

Sir,

This letter comes to you in my place. I'm too ashamed to go to see you. Besides, I don't have the money for the trip, because I'm no longer a teacher. I've been fired.

Last Friday, I loved a girl—or, as you would put it, I committed adultery—at least that's what the whites call it and the Church, too. But the girl wasn't married, nor had any bride-price been paid for her. Consequently she didn't belong to anyone and I don't understand who it is that I have wronged. I myself am unwed and I have no intention of marrying the girl. I don't even know her name. So, the way I see it, the commandment, "You shall not commit adultery" does not apply in my case. That's why I can't understand why the Church deprives me of Communion by putting me under discipline for six months.

One of my pupils told on me. And now I don't know where to turn.

Sir, you baptized me and taught me at school. You have counseled me often and know how I became a Christian. You know me even better than my own father does. I'm terribly sorry to disappoint you, but at the same time I tell you frankly, I don't feel very guilty. I'm ashamed because of all the talk about it, but I'm still a Christian.

I dare to tell you openly what I think even if you get angry. Aren't the desires of my body supposed to be satisfied? Aren't my sex organs given me to be used? Shouldn't you take advantage of that which is available? Why is it a sin to use what God has made?

Since everyone condemns me, I do not expect an answer. I will stop now, There's nothing more to be said.

Sincerely,
Your unhappy François

B. . . . . , January 19

My dear François,

I got your letter and I'm thankful you told me what happened before I heard it from someone else. Of course I'm sad. It's embarrassing for me too, because it was partly on my recommendation that you were given your job as a teacher.

But I'm not at all angry with you for being frank. Rather, I'm deeply moved by it, for then perhaps I can help you. May I answer your questions just as frankly as you have asked them?

Let us put aside for a moment the question of whether or not your case should be called adultery. You are absolutely right in saying that sex is no sin. Your desires, your thoughts when seeing a beautiful girl are not yet sin; neither is it sin if you feel attracted. You can't avoid physical desires any more than you can avoid having the birds fly around your head. But you can certainly prevent them from building nests in your hair.

Indeed, sexual desires are created by God. They are a gift of God, one of the most precious gifts you have received for your young life. But the existence of a desire does not justify its satisfaction. The presence of a power does not imply that one should be guided by it, blindly and without restraint.

What would you say about a fellow who stands in front of the window of a butcher's shop in a big city and reasons as follows: "Now that I see this meat, I'm hungrier than ever. The meat arouses my appetite. That proves it's meant for me and that I should have it. Therefore I have the right to smash the window and help myself."

You ask if that which exists should not be used. Yes, but only in its own time and place. Just imagine, for instance, that one of your friends has become a policeman. For the first time in his life he possesses a revolver. Now he says to himself: "I didn't acquire this revolver myself. It was given to me. Because it was given to me it should be used. Therefore I must shoot somebody with it—no matter whom."

No, he does not have this right. If the revolver has been given him, then he is responsible for its proper use.

The same is true about sex. It should be used, but in its proper place and time, according to God's plan. Within that plan the sexual instinct is a good thing, a powerful source of life and unity between two beings. Outside of God's plan, it quickly becomes a means of division, a source of cruelty, perversion and death.

I could say it also this way: Within God's will, sexual union fulfills its purpose only when it is an expression of love.

One phrase in your letter struck me especially. You wrote, "I loved a girl." No, my friend. You did not love that girl; you went to bed with her—these are two completely different things. You had a sexual episode, but what love is, you did not experience.

It's true you can say to a girl, "I love you," but what you really mean is something like this: "I want something. Not you, but something from you. I don't have time to wait. I want it immediately, without delay. It doesn't matter what happens afterwards. Whether we remain together, whether you become pregnant—that has nothing to do with me. For me, it's right now that counts. I will make use of you in order to satisfy my desire. You are for me only the means by which I can reach my goal. I want to have it—have it without any further ado, have it, immediately."

This is the opposite of love, for love wants *to give.* Love seeks to make the other one happy, and not himself. You acted like a pure egoist. Instead of saying: "I loved a girl," you should have said: "I loved myself and myself only. For this purpose I misused a girl."

Let me try to tell you what it really should mean if a fellow says to a girl, "I love you." It means: "You, you, you. You alone. You shall reign in my heart. You are the one whom I have longed for; without you I am incomplete. I will give everything for you and I will give up everything for you, myself as well as all that I possess. I will live for you alone, and I will work for you alone. And I will wait for you—it doesn't matter how long. I will always be patient with you. I will never force you, not even by words. I want to guard you, protect you and keep you from all evil. I want to share with you my thoughts, my heart and my body—all that I possess. I want to listen to what you have to say. There is nothing I want to undertake without your blessing. I want to remain always at your side."

Do you understand now how far removed your experience was from an experience of love? You don't even know the name of the girl. For you, she wasn't even a person, not even a number. You're not interested in her past, and certainly not in her future. You didn't even care what happened in her heart when you possessed her. And if she became pregnant—that's her affair. What does it matter to you?

No, you did not love her. True love involves responsibility—the one for the other and both before God. Where love is, you no longer say "I," but "you"; "I am responsible for you. You are responsible for me." Together then you stand before God where you do not say "you and I," but rather "we."

Only in marriage does this "we" become a full reality. Only in marriage can love really unfold and mature, because only there can it find permanence and faithfulness. True love never can and never will end. That's why you should use the great words, "I love you" very sparingly. You should save it for the girl whom you intend to marry.

Here in marriage is the right place to use your sexual powers. There they will help you to love your wife. They are one expression—one among many others—by means of which you make her understand how much you love her.

If you use your sexual powers apart from this kind of love, you are preparing yourself for an unhappy marriage.

Let me close here. This letter will give you enough to think about. Please remember that in spite of everything you can count always on my friendship and prayers.

Hoping for another frank letter from you,

Sincerely yours,
T.

M. . . . . , January 25

Dear Sir,

Your letter has reached me. Thank you very much for it. I'm grateful that you do not give me up. You criticize me severely, but you help me too. I'm very glad that I have found in you someone to whom I can write frankly, but I must admit I didn't understand everything you said to me. What surprised me the most was what you said at the end of the letter.

Sir, if I did have a true motive for my action, it was precisely that of preparing myself for a happy marriage. But now you tell me just the opposite. I ask you, sir, how can one know without first learning? How can one learn without experimenting? Didn't we do the same thing in our chemistry and physics classes?

In my mother tongue we have a proverb which says: "One must sharpen the spear before one goes hunting."

What use is it to be married if one is impotent because of not having trained sufficiently the powers of his body? Isn't there even a danger that the organs will remain underdeveloped if they are not used?

Do you understand what I mean? I hope you will find time to answer me once again.

François

B. . . . . , February 3

My dear François,

Thank you again for writing so honestly. I take it as a sign of your confidence.

There's a strange comparison between love and death in the Bible which says: "Love is strong as death" (Song of Solomon 8:6). Both love and death have this in common that you cannot try them out beforehand. But just that is what makes both of these experiences so powerful. Do you think you could try out what it feels like to be dead by sleeping very deeply? Even less can you try out what it feels like to be in love by a mere sexual contact. The conditions under which love can be experienced are so much higher, so much different.

Take another comparison: If you want to try out a parachute, you will be tempted perhaps to jump down from the top of a house or a high tree. But a distance of thirty or forty feet is not enough to give the parachute a chance to open up; therefore you may very well break your neck. You have to jump out of an airplane up several thousand feet if you want the parachute to open up and carry you to safety without mishap.

The same is true with love. You cannot try it outside the "high flight" of marriage. Only then can its wonders really unfold. Only then can the sexual organs function as they are meant to function.

When one is married, the sex act takes place under completely different conditions. There is no hurry, no fear of being discovered, no fear of being betrayed or left in the lurch by the other, no fear of a pregnancy resulting from it. But above all there is enough time to open your hearts and get used to one another, to correct together lovingly the awkwardness and minor difficulties which are always there at the beginning.

It is good, François, that you want to prepare yourself for marriage. But what is most important here is not the physical functioning of the sex organs. What matters is the *psychological* adjustment—in other words, the meeting of the hearts and minds of the two partners.

If there are sexual problems in marriage, it is not necessarily because of physical difficulties. These can be revealed and corrected before marriage by medical examinations. No, a far more common source of trouble is that very lack of psychological adjustment, which I have just mentioned.

Have you ever heard an orchestra tune its instruments before a concert? First comes the oboes, the violins and the flutes. If the conductor started with trumpets and drums which make a great deal of noise, he wouldn't be able to hear the oboes and violins and flutes. It's the same in the orchestra of marriage. The adjustment of heart and mind corresponds to the tuning of woodwinds and strings; then later the drums and trumpets of sex can be sounded.

It's this delicate tuning that you must learn if you want to prepare for marriage. This is what must be trained. But you are certainly not doing that when you have sexual relations with just any girl. Instead you are making your own heart numb. The drums drown out the flutes and you deaden your own feelings. What you have to be afraid of is not the underdevelopment of the sex organs, but the underdevelopment of love.

If you prepare yourself for marriage by having intercourse without this love, then, at best, you are imitating outwardly only some of its phases. You lower the sexual act to something machine-like, something bestial, for your heart is insensitive. You miss the decisive experience, the opening up of the "I" to the "you," and you block your-self from being able to love your future wife as deeply and as fully as she will expect you to.

Did it ever occur to you that sexual adventures before marriage can awaken in you a polygamous desire, a taste for variety, which may endanger your future marriage in advance? You may acquire wrong habits which will be very difficult to get rid of. Serious sexual handicaps, such as impotence, which can threaten the happiness of your marriage, can result.

When I as a pastor am called in for counsel in a marriage crisis, I can almost trace the origin of the problems to the kind of life which the husband and wife lived before they were married. The young man who has not learned self-control before marriage will not have it during marriage; so you see that your case does have something to do with marriage. In a sense, you deprive your future wife of something, even if you do not yet know her, and you endanger your happiness together.

My dear François, I hope you will understand at least one thing. I am not trying to deprive you of a pleasure, but rather I would like to protect you so that you will not spoil one of the greatest joys of your life. If you pick the blossoms of an orange tree, you will never know the taste of its fruit. So, when I advise you not to pick flowers, I do it not to take something away from you, but to assure you of a reward even more fulfilling.

May I answer your African proverb with another: "In trying to make himself too rich, a man often makes himself poor."

With brotherly greetings,
T.

M. . . . . , February 10

Dear Pastor,

While I was reading your last letter, a Bible verse came
to my mind which I have heard many times but which now
through our correspondence has taken on a new meaning:
"There is no fear in love, but perfect love casts out fear.
For fear has to do with punishment, and he who fears is
not perfected in love" (I John 4:18).

Yes, that is true. I was afraid, and to tell you the truth, I
had very little joy the night I was with that girl. But do you
know, it was also fear which drove me to do it—the fear of
becoming ill if too much semen were to accumulate in my
loins. Sometimes during the night I have dreams which
cause emissions. My comrades tell me that the only way to
escape these troubles is to try to have intercourse with a
girl. What do you think about that?

You warned me against awakening a polygamous desire
within me. Is it not possible to love several women at the
same time? There is no passage in the Bible which forbids
polygamy.

I have revealed to you my most secret thoughts in this
letter. I hope you are not too shocked. But I have no one
with whom I can talk about these problems, not even my
own parents. As far as medical examination goes, I would
have little confidence in it. Our doctors do not always tell
us the truth, because they are afraid of palavers with our
families.

Thank you again for your patience.

Yours sincerely,
François

B. . . . . , February 20

Dear Brother,

Let me start with your last question: No, I do not believe that one can love several women at the same time. Everything depends upon what you mean by the term "love." If "love" means to lie with a girl; if love is nothing but sex, you are right. But "perfect Love," which the Bible talks about in the verse you quoted, concerns not only the senses but the heart as well.

I'm sure you know this proverb: "In a heart where there is room for several, there is no room for one alone." This is true. Balzac once said: "To believe that it's impossible always to love the marriage partner alone is just as absurd as the supposition that a musician needs many instruments before he can produce a beautiful melody." The complete responsibility for the partner, as I've already explained, you can only assume for one woman.

You say that polygamy is not forbidden in the Bible. It would take too long to go into detail here about how the Bible treats this problem. Very briefly let me say this much. Even in the Old Testament, polygamy was not the rule, but the exception. Adam, Noah, Isaac, Joseph had only one wife as did all the prophets. Where polygamy occurs it is motivated almost always by childlessness. However the Bible is very realistic in pointing out clearly the troubles and disadvantages polygamy brings about—jealousy (Genesis 16:4), grief (Genesis 26:34), favoritism (Genesis 49:4). The Hebrew word for the second wife means "rival."

But the Bible does more than forbid. It gives us a positive definition of marriage from which we can draw our own conclusions. It says: "Therefore a man leaves his father and mother and cleaves to his wife (singular), and they (*two*) become one flesh." The expression "one flesh" can also be translated by "one living being," or better still, "one person."

In marriage man and wife are no longer two, but one. It is a joining of two persons into "one flesh" in such a way that the two become one and yet remain distinct. This marriage-person has two essential organs: the "head" and the "heart." The man might be said to be the head, the wife the heart. Both are equally important for the life of the marriage-person, which is not able to live without a head or a heart, nor if it has two heads or two hearts. There must be just one head and one heart.

This means that if you are a polygamist, your marriage may still be a marriage, but you and your wives are not "one person"; and you together can never be an "image" of God. This was God's purpose when He created man: "God created man in his own image. . . . In His own image created He them, man and wife" (Genesis 1:27). In polygamy there can be no marriage-person, who can become the partner of God. Nor can such a marriage be a mirror where the mutual love between man and wife reflects God's "perfect love." Only monogamy can testify to God's love.

What your friends have told you is a plain lie. No one has ever fallen ill because of continence before marriage. Emissions during sleep are not a sign of illness, but a sign that your body is functioning normally. It's all a part of God's creation that the body gets rid automatically of that which it does not use. That is all. There is nothing mysterious, nothing unnatural behind it.

On the contrary, if you go to bed with just any kind of girl you run the great danger of catching a venereal disease, or of becoming impotent for psychological reasons.

Those who tell you that you must have intercourse in order to avoid falling ill, or to prove that you are normal, are usually those who have thought up this excuse because they are not able to exercise control over themselves.

Please be assured, François, that none of the thoughts you share with me, nor any question you ask, will shock me. My heart goes out to the many young people today who suffer inwardly, because they must live alone with their problems. If only they could be encouraged to open their hearts to someone who could counsel with them!

I greet you as your brother in Christ. He is the perfect example of God's "perfect love," and He loves you no matter what.

Yours sincerely,
T.

M. . . . . , February 28

Dear Pastor T.,

I write to you with growing joy, because I feel that I am no longer left alone, and that gives me new courage.

In your last letter you mentioned that one could catch a disease or become impotent by sleeping with just any girl. That is strange—it was precisely in order to prove that I'm not impotent, that I did what I did. I'll tell you the whole story now without hiding anything.

On that unlucky day, one of my friends invited me to visit his parents. It was toward evening. While we were on the way to his house he started to tease me. He told me that I was not really a man if I had never known a girl. When we arrived at his home, his parents were not there; only his sister was in the house. We started to talk and she served us some beer. Suddenly my friend disappeared and I was left alone with the girl.

She invited me, and when I refused she began to make fun of me. Above all, she called me a word which translated means "dishrag" and which we use in our tribal language to describe a man who is both cowardly and impotent.

Sir, perhaps you as a white man cannot imagine what such a term means to an African. To be called impotent is one of the greatest insults a man can suffer in our society. If I had not given her the proof of my powers she would have slandered my name everywhere.

To tell you the truth, I certainly did not "love" the girl in the sense which you give to that word. Deep down in my heart perhaps I even hated her. But there was nothing else that I could do, the fear of being mocked and becoming the object of gossip was stronger than any other fear.

Tell me, how can you be a man and have the reputation of being a man unless you act like a man?

Yours sincerely,
F.

B. . . . . , March 6

Dear Brother,

I'm glad that at last you have told me the whole story just as it happened. So what drove you to do it was not really the worry about your health nor the noble desire to prepare yourself for marriage, as you have pretended, but simply the fear of mockery, of being made a laughing-stock. That makes it easy for me to answer your last question.

You did not behave like a man; you behaved instead exactly like a dishrag. A man who is a man knows what he wants, makes a decision and then acts upon it. But to let yourself be made to act against your own will by the words of a girl proves that you were a coward. In my view, when you stop to think about it, I should think you would find what you did more humiliating than putting up with the mockery of the whole village.

Even in going to your friend's house, you did not act like a man. A man must be smart enough to foresee such traps. The conversation with your friend on the way should have made you suspicious. The alcohol weakened your powers of resistance. In such a situation the act of true courage is to flee.

No, you did not act like a man. A man does not let himself be pushed around. He is his own master.

I remember one day when our youth group went on a hike. After a long walk which made us very thirsty we came to a spring of clear, cool water. Our leader made us wait beside it for half an hour before we could drink. He did that to teach us self-control.

Not to resist temptation, but to satisfy every desire the moment you feel it will make you soft, a man without a backbone, whom serious girls will not respect. If a girl turns you down because you won't take her immediately, then she isn't the girl for you. Girls who are worthy of their name deep down in their hearts want only one thing: a real man and nothing less than a man.

If you want to prove that you are a man—not merely a male animal—then, as in driving a car, you must learn first of all how to use the brakes and the steering wheel. The gas pedal is easy enough to manipulate. The brakes are something else again. Not to let go, but rather to control is the sign of true manhood. All through marriage you will need this self-control; for example, when your wife is sick, or troubled, or when you must be separated because one or the other must be away.

Now you'll probably say: "It isn't easy to become a man." That's true, my friend, it isn't easy. In fact it's extremely difficult to master this young new power which breaks out within you. It's a battle, above all to resist the temptation to satisfy your desire alone by yourself. When this temptation comes over you, then remember this: *the sex instinct is given us as a means of communion.* To satisfy it by yourself means to abuse it, because it isolates you and makes you seek in yourself a satisfaction that is to be received in communion with another. For this reason it turns you in upon yourself while the real act of love should open you to your partner. Performing the act alone leaves an aftertaste of defeat, shame and emptiness.

Nevertheless, if you should come to the point of giving in to this, do not feel that you are perverted, abnormal and condemned, nor should you look upon it as a tragedy. The battle is really difficult only as long as you think of yourself as your own master. Everything will be easier when you realize that your body belongs to God and He has entrusted to you your sexual powers, as well as your talents, your time and your money to be used for the happiness of your fellow men.

The more you learn this sexual self-control, the greater will become your ability to love with the heart. You will learn to recognize the kind of love that is aroused by a smile or a gesture or a certain tone of voice and which reveals the heart of a girl. This is very soft music and you need practice in order to hear it. The more you tone down the drums, the more you will become aware of it.

Sexual control is like a kerosene lamp. If you do not manage the wick properly, the flame will leap too high, the glass will be darkened with smoke and the lamp will give no light. You have to adjust the wick for the lamp to give proper light.

There is no art without skill. Since love is an art, it needs skill. But every skill has to be learned and no skill can be without discipline.

It is a great help, until the time when you can use your sexual power for the happiness of the one whom God has destined for you, to find an outlet for this power in some creative activity. Write, paint or even compose music! Look for friends who stimulate and challenge you. Devote yourself to work which you enjoy, or to a hobby which demands your best. How would it be to learn a craft, or to play some musical instrument; to take a trip through your own country or beyond its borders? These will offer you excellent opportunities to transmute your desires and to use your masculine strength for a constructive purpose.

Above all, don't remain alone in this struggle. If I can, I should like to be a good friend to you in it. But don't forget that the best friend in any trouble is Jesus Christ Himself.

Now a final word about the fear of mockery. Your Lord was mocked; they even spat in His face. Why are you then afraid of being laughed at by a girl?

Jesus Christ, the man of God, is the only one who can make a man of you.

In Him,
T.

M. . . . . , March 12

Dear Pastor T.,

You certainly hit me right between the eyes in your last letter. Perhaps I was too much afraid of that girl and her scorn.

On the other hand, I still think that it's necessary to know what a woman is like before you marry.

In my tribe one hears often about women who "have water"; women with whom it is impossible to carry out the sex act. It certainly cannot be a sin to find that out before marriage. Wouldn't it also be a favor to the girl? We have a proverb which says, "a woman who has water rarely bears a child." Shouldn't a man know before marriage whether a girl is able to have children, so that he will not be tempted to take a second wife later?

You said that you wanted to be a good friend to me, so I have the nerve to ask these questions without beating around the bush.

I wait impatiently for your next letter.

Yours,
F.

B. . . . . , March 18

My dear friend,

The questions you asked in your last letter are very important. Before I go on I want to thank you for asking them so clearly and bluntly. They help me to clarify my own thinking.

Yes, I know there are many people who think that the happiness of a marriage depends upon the structure of the female sex organs. But first of all, you must realize that it's not a question of bones, but of very flexible organs and tender tissues which, in the course of a marriage, adjust themselves. As far as the anatomy itself is concerned, you can learn more by reading a marriage manual than you can from a sexual experiment. If there is a physical abnormality then only a medical examination can reveal it with certainty.

The same holds true about the myth of "women with water." I've heard talk about this problem and I'm still not sure what to think about it. But one thing that strikes me though is that I've never yet met a man who has seen such a case himself. I've talked with both European and African doctors who have worked for many years in Africa and they all say that never yet have they examined a woman with such a condition.

In any case, it is absolute foolishness to lie with just any girl in order to know what women are like. There's no such thing, you know, as a typical woman, for every woman is different, not only her body, but her heart. Every person is unique. After five minutes with a girl in the bush, you know very little about her body, and absolutely nothing about her mind and heart.

The word "know" is a great word. The Hebrew word for it used in the Bible means "to know someone by name." In other words, to know someone very well, to take care of that one, to love and to respect him or her as a person. The Bible uses this word for the first time in Genesis 4:1, "Adam knew Eve, *his* wife." You can never know what *the* woman or *a* woman is like; you can only know *your* wife. That means you cannot know a woman except in marriage, in the atmosphere of faithfulness, where the sex act is one of the expressions of love.

Do you have to take a risk then? To a certain extent, yes. Marriage is a risk. Otherwise it would be a bore. But this risk is probably less than you think, so long as love is free to work its miracle. The fact that you say you're doing a favor to the girl when you try her out shows me that you have no idea what happens in her heart when she has a sexual experience. A girl cannot separate the sensations of her body from her heart and soul as a young man may do. Emotionally, she is moved much more deeply, and the impression of the first man to whom she has given herself will remain with her. She can never dismiss him from her mind completely even if she hates him later, even if she eventually marries someone she really loves. And even for the young man, the first girl whom he has possessed will always remain his to some extent. May she be his in reality.

Most of the time a girl, under the stress of emotion, is not altogether mindful of what she is risking. It is up to the man to know it for her. I hope you can see now that to respect a girl's virginity before marriage has much more to it than just being the narrow-minded idea of some old-fashioned people. Her very nature requires it. Therefore a time of great responsibility begins when you meet a girl. You must always keep in mind how dangerous it is for her to give herself too soon. You must realize what serious consequences this act can have, even though she seems ready to give in—yes, even though she be the one who takes the lead. Such awareness will make it easier for you to master your desire. Only by maintaining an attitude of chivalry are you really doing the girl "a favor."

You don't even have to consider the commandment, "You shall not commit adultery." You don't have to question whether or not you have broken it. To keep Jesus' commandment, "You shall love your neighbor as yourself," which He called the greatest of all commandments, would certainly mean to abstain from pre-marital relations; for you would be hurting your neighbor instead of loving her as yourself.

Sincerely,

T.

M. . . . . , March 26

Dear Pastor,

What you told me in your last letter was completely new to me. It never entered my mind that in possessing a girl who invited me to do so, I was doing her a wrong. I always thought I would be pleasing her.

I've talked to some of my friends about this. But they think that it would still be permitted and even an advantage to have experiences with girls who are used to it, who are already in a sense "spoiled" and to whom you could do no harm. I'd like to know what you think about this arrangement.

You didn't yet answer my question about the wife who can bear no children. Shouldn't you find out for sure before marriage whether or not a woman is fertile, in order not to have the temptation later on to take another wife who would be able to bear children. For marriage without children certainly doesn't make sense.

Yours,

F.

B. . . . . , March 30

My dear François,

Please forgive me that I overlooked the question in your last letter about a childless marriage. But first a word about the arguments of your friends.

If you get involved in a sexual experience with a girl who does not have marriage in mind, you don't have a true woman as your partner.

Alexandre Dumas has said: "If you have a sexual experience with a girl worthy of you, you do damage to her. If you have it with a girl unworthy of you, you do damage to yourself."

In your tribe I have heard that originally intercourse before marriage was punished, often very severely. That's why I wonder whether your ancestors too did not already know some of these truths. What do you think?

But however that might be, God's will is never without reason. God knows better than you do the conditions which make for your happiness. He does not cheat you when he wants you to have only *your* wife, when He does not want you to "know" another woman before your own wife.

It's really strange. All the young men that I know want to marry virgins. But on the other hand they want to experiment first. Who can know when he "spoils" someone else's fiancée whether his own will not be treated in the same way? Don't you see how contradictory it is?

That leads to your question about childless marriages. This problem is closely connected with promiscuity. I have often wondered why the number of sterile couples— for the man can also be sterile—is constantly growing in

Africa. Doctors are in agreement that the main cause is so much intercourse before marriage. Such conduct encourages the spread of venereal diseases, which doctors tell me is the most common cause of sterility. Many girls will not become mothers and many young men will never become fathers because of their experimentation before marriage.

In connection with this I would like to tell you something that is not yet widely known in Africa. Normally the conception of a child can take place only when the ovum separates itself from the ovary of the woman. This is usually between the nineteenth and fourteenth day before her next menstrual period. The choice of a day favorable to fertilization is therefore very important. But I'd like to say again: every woman is different and you can only find out this day for your wife in the course of your marriage. Experimenting before marriage does not help you here at all.

Even with all our modern knowledge of bodily functioning, and all our medical skills children remain a gracious gift of God. The one to whom God does not grant this gift must realize that children, in and of themselves, are not the sole objects of marriage. According to the Bible, the union of husband and wife in one single being is a complete fulfillment. Also, you may have noticed how often God uses childless couples to carry out some great task for which they would not have been available if they had children.

But we can talk about that later if you should ever find yourself in this situation. For the moment it's enough if you realize this: many girls in Africa are afraid that their husbands would divorce them or take wives if they as wives do not bear children. The fear of barrenness is of itself enough to make a girl childless. That is why you should leave no doubt in the heart of your fiancée as to your love for her. She must know for sure that you love her, just as she is, completely, whether she bears you a child or not.

These are the pledges you will make to your wife before God on your wedding day:

I promise to love you and comfort you,
honor and keep you, in sickness and in health;
and forsaking all others keep only unto you so long
as we both shall live.

The most important decision of your life is the decision to follow Jesus Christ. The second most important decision is your choice of a marriage partner. May God guide you!

In Christ,

T.

M. . . . . , April 4

My dear Pastor,

Why has no one ever told me this before? Neither with my parents, nor with our catechist, nor with our African pastor have I ever talked over these matters. The only recollection I have of this subject is a sermon against adultery by an American missionary which I heard when I was ten years old and which raised many questions in my mind. But when I asked my father about them, he beat me.

Now I am being punished as a guilty person and put "under discipline," without anyone taking the trouble to explain to me why I am guilty. When I have finished these six months in which I am barred from Communion, is everything automatically in order again? Can I be certain that God has forgiven me?

And still another question. I think I can see now that having hasty relationships with any girl who happens to be handy is of no real help in getting to know what a woman is like. But in order to marry, you have to choose first. How can you make a choice without getting acquainted with girls? Where and how can I meet girls? Where should I go? Where should I not go? What do you think about dancing? Why is it that all girls imagine that as soon as a fellow approaches them he has nothing else in mind but having sexual relations?

Finally, if you say that the physical aspect is not sufficient as a guide for the choosing, what then are the standards I should have in making my choice? How can I ever know whether a girl loves me or whether I love a girl?

Nothing but questions! Hoping that you will not lose patience with me.

Yours,

F.

B. . . . . , April 15

My dear François,

You are absolutely right. You must get acquainted with girls before you can choose. But it's still a little difficult for me to give advice that can be put into practice here in Africa. The existence of love in the Christian sense—that is, the free and mutual giving between two persons—is still not widely recognized. In former times, girls were strictly guarded and often were "married" from the time they were born, sometimes even before.

The attitudes that grew out of these customs are still alive and you cannot change them quickly. But I think the time has come to take some steps in a new direction. In order to make happy marriages possible, we must create opportunities where girls and fellows can meet and be together as good comrades, without embarrassment or false shame, under conditions in which they learn to respect one another. Coeducational schools, youth groups, work camps during vacations: all these would offer such opportunities. There would be a real undertaking for the Church, not to stop with preaching against adultery, but to create conditions for a healthy relationship between the sexes by organizing youth centers in towns and villages.

You ask: "Where is it good for me to go?" It is difficult to give you any hard and fast rules. It is above all a matter of atmosphere. You must use your own judgment as to where and when you may dance. It is up to you to see the danger in public dance halls. It is up to you to avoid getting involved in situations from which you will not know how to escape.

One good rule is to say to yourself simply: "I will not go where I should not want to be seen by the one whom I respect and love more than anyone else in the world."

That girls suspect sexual intentions from the fellow comes partly from custom, partly from their unfortunate experiences. It's up to you to act differently. I'm sure that girls who are to be taken seriously also welcome the opportunity to meet you as friends. If a girl is sincere you will win her respect and confidence by your good conduct. This should be your aim: to become a young man who is chivalrous; in other words, of all your friends, to be the one who has the greatest respect and consideration for girls.

Naturally, the day will come when you have to make a choice. You must not take this decision lightly, as if it could be changed later on. In God's view marriage cannot be broken. Nothing but death can separate those of whom Jesus declares: "They are no more two but one. . . . Those whom God has joined together, let no man put asunder."

As a guide for your choice, it might be wise to ask these questions:

(1) First, the question of faith. I see from your last letter that God's forgiveness is important to you. That means you cannot imagine living your life without Jesus Christ. That's why your first question should be: "Is the girl a Christian? Can I pray with her?" Being one in faith is the foundation for becoming one in marriage.

(2) You should then ask yourself: "Do I really love her?" You must know that. But how can you know that? Here are some of the signs: If you cannot imagine living your life without her; if you feel pain when you are away from her; if she occupies your thoughts, and inspires your dreams at all times; if her happiness means more to you than your own. Similarly, there are signs that you can look for when a girl loves you: if she writes often to you, if she tries to please you, if she looks for excuses to meet you. A most significant sign is her breaking off of friendships with other young men.

(3) It is not enough to love her as a sister if she is to become your wife. You have to be *in* love with her as a woman. Ask yourself: "Do I want her to be the mother of my children?" You will find out that when you ask yourself this question many girls who please you only because of their superficial good looks are automatically eliminated from your choice. In the same way a girl should ask herself: "Am I ready to give myself to him? Do I want to become the mother of his children?" She will not want to give her children a father who is a heavy drinker, undisciplined, bad-tempered, irresponsible, selfish, stingy or lazy.

(4) Is she one who, by her conduct and attitude, by her likes and dislikes, by her character and interests as well as by her education and ability, will be able to help me in fulfilling my vocation? Is she one who can share with me the sorrows and joys of my work and who will stand by my side as a true companion when these joys and sorrows come? That's why in your case, I think you should look for a girl who has at least some education, so that you can talk over with her the problems of your work as a teacher. This is absolutely necessary. True love communicates. Love that finds no words to express itself soon dies.

There are also two or three other questions which you can ask yourself—about her health, about her social background, about her age. It's better that your wife be a little bit younger than you, but not too much. According to my doctor friends, the ideal age for a young man to marry is twenty-five and for the girl twenty-one. But this is only a guiding principle rather than a stiff rule.

Don't marry simply to please someone in your family. Never look upon a woman as a means to an end—any end. Love her for her own sake and not for the gain she will bring you.

However these are all only some human counsels. Every marriage is a unique experience, filled with the unknown and unexpected, a dangerous but a magnificent adventure. Only with confidence in God can you dare to set out on this adventure.

In other words, God must guide you. It is at this point where your question about the choice of a wife touches your question about forgiveness. As long as you have not received His forgiveness, God cannot guide you. By transgressing His commandments we separate ourselves from Him. It's as if there were a telephone wire between God and ourselves. When we sin, the wire becomes disconnected. Only when the connection is working can we hear God's voice.

To repair this connection is not as easy as you seem to think: Six months "church discipline" and then "automatically" to obtain forgiveness? No, the grace of God is not so cheap. It requires you to admit your fault and to repent in your heart.

Church discipline shall testify to the world that the church does not approve of this or that behavior. But it can never replace repentance, and neither can it be a punishment. It is not up to the Church to punish sin. That would be to insult Jesus Christ, who took our punishment by dying for us on the cross. "He was wounded for our transgressions, he was bruised for our iniquities; upon him was the punishment that made us whole, and with his stripes we are healed." (Isaiah 53:5)

I invite you to read, slowly, and several times over, Psalm 32. One of the mysteries of the Christian life is revealed there: the relationship between our repentance and the fact that God guides us.

The Psalmist says: "When I declared not my sin, my body wasted away." And he adds: "I acknowledge my sin to Thee." God answers: "I will instruct you and teach you in the way you should go."

I already know what question you will ask in your next

letter: "How can I repent?" This is indeed the key question in life, the answer to which comprises the answers to all other questions.

I cannot, however, give this answer by letter. We've now arrived at a certain boundary in our correspondence. So far I have been able to advise you by writing. But now we need to talk together as brother to brother. That is why I invite you to come and visit me.

No one can tell the Gospel to himself. We need a brother who proclaims it to us. Dietrich Bonhoeffer, one of the great theologians of our time, has expressed this truth as follows: "Christ became our brother in order to help us; now, through Him, our brother becomes for us a 'Christ' with all the authority of this commission. Our brother stands before us as a symbol of the truth and grace of God. He is given to us as a help. He bears our confession of sin in the place of Christ, and he forgives us our sin in Christ's name."

I am ready and waiting for you.

Your brother in Christ,
T.

P.S. Make this experiment and come. Enclosed is a money order for your travel expenses.

E. . . . . , May 2

Dear brother in Christ,

This is just to let you know that I had a good journey home. Almost too good. But I shall tell you about that later.

First of all my thanks for your spiritual help. Now I can admit what a great effort it was for me to come to you at all. I did not intend to do it. But when you sent me the money for the trip, you took away my best excuse. I had made up my mind not to say anything and to let you do the talking. I confess that I was afraid. The hearing before the church elders hardly bothered me at all. But to come to see you, that was hard for me.

Everything was so completely different from what I had expected. You never gave me the impression that I was standing before a judge. Rather, it was like sitting with a brother who was also a sinner.

The fact that you talked so frankly about your own defeats encouraged me to speak freely about my own. At first I wanted to do it like the farmer who admitted to his pastor that he had stolen a rope. Weeks later the pastor met him again. Still the farmer looked unhappy. So the pastor asked him: "Was there something tied on to the rope?" "Yes," he said, "a cow." I don't know how it happened, but all at once it was easy for me to talk also about the "cow." I never dreamed what a relief it is simply to speak out certain things. It's something that you can't know until you have "experimented."

Unfortunately the "cow" which was the reason for writing my first letter to you was not my only one. It took a great effort for me to reveal it to you. But strangely enough, you and I didn't become more dejected by speaking of these things. Instead we grew always happier. We even laughed. At the end the atmosphere was actually gay. Perhaps such a conversation is actually the happiest thing in the world. I noticed, too, that the main thing was not my fall, but rather my getting up again; not my sins, but rather the forgiveness of those sins.

You are right. It's impossible to confess your sins to yourself. In my best hours I had tried to persuade myself that God had forgiven me. But I had real assurance of it for the first time when we prayed together and then you announced it to me so personally by quoting Isaiah 43:1: "François, fear not; François, I have redeemed you; François, I have called you by your name; François, you are mine."

Sometimes it's hard for me to believe that the punishment which I have deserved is carried by Jesus and that this thought shall give me peace. Sometimes I think it would give me more peace to suffer—at least a little—for what I have done; not to earn forgiveness, but to show my repentance through action. But, as you said, this may be merely pride. I shall try to believe that Jesus has done everything.

But now you shall hear what happened to me on my return trip. My head is swimming. I'm all confused. I'm beside myself with joy. I am . . . I don't know what. . . . To be brief, I got acquainted with a girl!

"Girl" is the wrong word. I should rather say, "queen." And what does it mean to "get acquainted"? I can only say this: for the first time in my life I have seen in a girl a human being, a person.

That such a meeting can change one so completely! It's impossible to believe. I don't know myself. I cannot possibly describe her to you. I cannot tell you how beautiful she is and why she is so perfect. Words seem pale, colorless, unworthy. Every expression is an understatement. Just this much I will say: I met the girl who will be my wife. Now I would like to see your face!

I still have a question though. It puzzles me that all this happened so soon after my visit with you. Do you think it is possible that God guided me in this experience? That there is a connection between this friendship and my confession?

You assured me that God would guide me in a new way after the "telephone line" was repaired. But so quickly? Is God so close? I tremble . . .

There's much more to tell you. But I must close. I want to write again to "her."

Your dazed F.

B. . . . . , May 6

My dear dazed François,

Thanks for your last letter which arrived today. Nothing could make me happier. Congratulations! If I understand you rightly, you are really in love. I thank God that He has given you this experience.

Yes, I'm quite sure that there is a connection between your new step in faith and the meeting with this girl. God does not always act so promptly. Sometimes He lets us wait a long time in order to teach us patience and in order to try our faith. If he has answered your prayers so quickly and so clearly, it must be for the purpose of encouraging you while you are taking the first faltering steps in the new life. But He is constantly at work and always close to you, whether you realize it or not. I hope that the tremor you feel in your heart will never leave you.

Now I am really curious and you must allow me to ask questions for once. Who is this girl? What's her name? Please tell me in detail how you became acquainted with this angel. Does she love you too? Have you already talked with her parents? May I perform the ceremony? Shall I start preparing a sermon?

Please answer soon!

Yours in curiosity,
T.

E. . . . . , June 3

My dear father in Christ,

Four weeks have gone by since I received your letter. No, sir, do not prepare any wedding sermon. It will be years before we can get married, if ever.

I am dreadfully unhappy.

But first of all let me tell you the whole story from the beginning. Her name is Cecile. We met each other in the bus. She had a baby in her arms. Later I learned that it was her sister's baby. Her sister was ill. I took her for a married woman. She had two suitcases and a bundle of pans beside her. We did not have seats. On the curves of the road we had to lean against each other to keep our balance. We talked about everyday things. My first impression was: "Here is a girl who is different." It's hard to explain. She was more open than others and yet at the same time more reserved.

When she reached her destination she asked me to pass her suitcases and bundle through the window. But the driver started the bus before I was able to give them to her. Five minutes went by before I could persuade him to stop again.

I got out then and found myself in the middle of nowhere with the baggage of a stranger. What should I do? I walked back. After twenty minutes I found the girl with the baby, both of them crying.

There was little hope of getting another ride the same day. So she invited me to stay with her parents in her village a couple of miles away from the road.

A strange situation. We arrived, she with the baby in her arms and the bundle of pans on her head, I with her two suitcases. Everyone in the village stood there staring at us.

A cool reception at first. She explained the situation. A good meal.

A thousand times I have asked myself the questions you ask. The answer to them all seems to be "yes." She is a Christian, a student, and she is interested in teaching. I cannot imagine anyone better fitted to become the mother of my children. She is a little younger than I am, and in good health. Besides that, I could sense that she was not indifferent to me. Even if she did not say anything, her eyes said a great deal.

The idea of inviting her for the night never even entered my head. Formerly that would have been my first thought. I don't know myself anymore.

I left the next morning and told her goodbye. Her parents were polite. But they did not say anything.

Then the letters came—almost every day. Here is one of them which I already know by heart. Please send it back to me as soon as you can. From it you will see what a serious-minded girl she is. I swim in happiness, am full of plans . . .

But then comes the bill.

No, I can't find another word for it. Her father wants to sell her, as at an auction, to the highest bidder. He asks for a payment of $400 in advance since, he claims, there are already other bids for her. But I'm afraid this will be only the beginning, the down payment, the first installment. I cry when I think it is my angel for sale, the one whom I love.

What do you say now? You didn't think of this big obstacle, did you? All the pretty things you said about the love of the heart and the soul. A lot of good they'll do me now, won't they?

Of course, no one can stop us from loving each other. Within the clan system to get married simply because we are in love is incredible and cannot be tolerated. Under this system, the girl is never the wife of her husband, but the wife of the bride-price.

Four hundred dollars! For me this is altogether out of the question, an impossible amount. You have made me dream. But reality is cruel and destroys that dream. I've ceased to hope.

Or would you like me to work for you as a washboy, until my hair is as white as the clothes I wash?

Look, I know that I am insolent and ungrateful. You have done nothing to deserve this tone I am taking with you. But I don't know any other way to give vent to my despair.

I would rather die than to just exist without really living. By that I mean, I guess you know, to exist without her. I want to cry aloud, cry out in the name of thousands of young men who are condemned to live without love, who are driven into the arms of prostitutes. I want to cry out in the name of thousands of girls who are forced into marriages with rich old men, who are often polygamous.

But who will hear my cry?

I accuse those who hold responsible positions in our country—those who dissipate with the money of the poor instead of breaking the monopoly which the rich hold on women, and abolishing this brutal and inhuman custom.

I accuse this totalitarian society, this dictatorship of the clan which uses the girl to balance the family budget and to fulfill the material wishes of her parents.

I accuse the selfish fathers who are too lazy to work and who use the money from selling their daughters to pay their debts, to buy alcohol, cars and wives.

I accuse the girls who remain passive when they come up against the curse of the bride-price instead of speaking out; who let their parents have their way and who only complain when their marriage becomes as much of a prison as though they were enclosed by stone walls or barbed wire.

I accuse the Church, which, instead of instructing me, placed me under harsh laws which I could not understand; and when I transgressed them and was more than ever in need of God's grace, deprived me of that grace. I accuse this Church which punishes instead of helping, and which takes away my job.

Why does God, the so-called protector of true marriage, show me His way without enabling me to walk in it? If the marriage of love remains the privilege of the rich, why doesn't God send me from heaven the $400 that I need? Where is His power? Is He not stronger than these little false gods—mammon and the clan? What a God!

You have awakened in me feeling of which I did not believe myself capable. You have taught me to love. You have kindled in my heart a fire of heavenly origin, without which I no longer consider myself a man. But now this fire consumes me. It makes me suffer more than I can bear, and it will kill me.

I do not expect an answer, for there is none.

Yours,

F.

To the Reader

I was speechless when I first read this letter from François. I really didn't know how I should react to it. In no case did I want to put him off with cheap cut-and-dried answers and empty promises or even ask him the somewhat malicious counter-question, whether he would have written the same letter if he were the father of marriageable daughters. I knew that behind this angry outcry of an African young man is the distress and anguish of thousands.

One must not weigh too heavily the words in such a letter and above all one must not be pushed to the defensive because of the bitterness of its tone and the injustice of its exaggerations. The first thing to do is simply to listen to this cry. That's why I decided that the best expression of my understanding and the most honest way to answer was just to be silent for the time being.

It is hard for us to realize that the same development which Western society has made in centuries, Africa is now making in decades. Originally the bride-price was a very meaningful custom which served to stabilize marriage. The goods involved were livestock and served as a recompense to the family of the girl for the loss of productive powers. In case of a divorce the cattle had to be returned. For that reason the girl's family was eager to preserve her marriage.

The introduction of money, which is paid today and spent tomorrow, to a large extent nullified the purpose of this custom. The availability of western luxury articles removed it one step further from its original purpose. Today, in many cases, you will find nothing short of a slave trade in girls. A prominent African lawyer once showed me shelves covering one wall of his office all filled with the records of lawsuits against fathers who had accepted money from different suitors for the same daughter.

The battlefield, however, on which this abrupt clash of old and new takes place is the human heart. There is no area of life which is more affected than that of marriage and the family. At this focal point all the social, religious and political problems of modern Africa appear to meet and become visible. Raising the status of women seems to be the basic condition for all further evolution in Africa. Man cannot be free as long as there is no free woman at his side. Political independence is not possible without independent and responsible couples. But there will be no independent couples as long as love is not the supporting foundation of marriage.

If this is true, then we stand with empty hands. If the key to the solution of Africa's problem lies in a deeper understanding of what love, in particular, married love, is, what do we have to offer? What does an African see in this area when he comes to Europe or America? Haven't we ourselves just begun to discover love as the supporting foundation of marriage? Even though we have no brideprice is not love menaced by other forms of materialism?

When I was this far along in my reflections I was able to put myself in François' place. The more we understand someone else, the more we learn to know ourselves. The same holds true for a continent. When we start to get the feel of Africa, we see suddenly our own country in a different light. We no longer stand there as condescending givers, as those who are advanced and mature, who know all the answers, but as those who are also in need of help.

This had just become clear to me, when I received the following letter from Cecile, which gave me new courage to fight for the marriage of François.

Y. . . . . , July 2

Dear Pastor T.,

I'm writing to you because I'm very upset. I haven't heard anything from François for almost four weeks.

He's spoken and written a great deal about you. That's why I dare to turn to you now.

Ever since I've been going to school in Y. we have written to each other almost every day. But since the beginning of June, he has not answered my letters.

I'm very worried. What shall I do? Can you help me?

Cecile

B. . . . . , July 10

Dear Cecile,

I'm happy that you wrote to me. From what François has written about you, I feel that I know you already, although we've never met.

François has been very close to my heart ever since he was a schoolboy. I'd like to suggest to you that we become a team in order to help him.

Perhaps you do not realize what it meant to him to get acquainted with you.

You know that he lost his job at the beginning of the year. He was really desperate when that happened, and we had a long and detailed correspondence about it. He felt that he had been abandoned by his church, and I was afraid that he would lose his faith completely.

Through a miracle, the opposite happened. His faith became deeper. He let himself be forgiven. That which God did for him was far greater than that which men did. He had the courage to become very small before God and that's why God could become very great to him. He threw himself into God's arms again.

That was a great moment. You must be thankful that you will receive a husband who has made such a decision.

On the way home he met you. Coincidence? For François it was more than that. It was for him a sign that God had not abandoned him. That God loved him in spite of everything. It strengthened his faith. It made it easier for him to trust in God, because he met you.

That's why it hit him all the harder when your father asked for $400 as the bride-price. Did you know anything about this?

When he received this news, his whole faith began to totter. He wrote me a raging letter, of which I'll send you a copy of the last part. It's a typical François-letter. You know him a little already. He has the tendency, as soon as an obstacle confronts him, to throw away everything: faith, love, God, state, church, me and even you.

This letter was written on June 3. Since then I haven't heart from François either.

Cecile, I've read this letter of his often and each time I feel anew: It's a great letter. He is so honest in his anger. François accuses everyone and everything—except himself. He acts as if he would be the first and only one who would have to pay the bride-price. But that's the way he is—our François. As long as something bothers others he doesn't let it get under his skin. But when it bothers him, he falls apart completely.

In no case should this letter remain unanswered. He's simply expressing what so many feel. I tell you honestly, that at first this letter left me speechless. I knew only too well that we Europeans are also to blame that a useful custom has become abused.

I was just thinking how I might answer in a helpful and effective way, when your letter arrived.

That's what gave me the following thought: At the moment you can help François more than I. That's why I'd like for you to answer the letter instead of me.

Let's become allies in the battle for your marriage. Show François that love is no forbidden land for Africans, as so many people think. Show him that Africans can— and may—love too.

This is not a question of money, but a question of faith. Show him that love does not accuse and denounce, but it fights.

Notice especially the paragraph in his letter in which he accuses the girls of remaining indifferent and passive before such a curse as the bride-price.

You're the only one who can answer this reproach. Show François that there are girls in Africa who are different, who dare to speak out.

I have great confidence in you, and I count on you.

Walter T.

Y. . . . . , July 20

Dear Pastor T.,

Yesterday I did what you asked and answered François' letter. I had to fight with myself for a long time. At first I didn't want to do it at all. Now I have at least tried. Enclosed you will see the result.

It was a difficult letter. I am still afraid to send it.

All last night I thought about what I should do. Then I got the idea of sending it to you first so you could look it over. Please read it to your wife as well. If she thinks that it is also good to send it, then I will.

It's so hard to be completely honest and still not to wound. I am afraid already of François' answer. Perhaps I should omit the last four words. Do you think they are too strong?

Cecile

Y. . . . . , July 19

Dear François,

I love a young man. His name is François. Please don't doubt that for a minute when you read this letter.

I was attracted to you from the first moment we met in the bus and then again when you helped me carry home my baggage. I felt even more drawn to you when you made no attempt that night to come to me. I felt then that you were not just interested in my body, but in myself. Not just in an hour of passion, but in a lifetime together.

It is because I love you I dare to write this frank letter to you.

Pastor Walter has quoted to me certain parts of the letter which you wrote to him on June 3. He has asked me to tell you what I think about it.

When I first read the letter, I was a little embarrassed— for you. But now I can at least understand why I have heard nothing from you for so long.

François, I understand you very well. I have kept all your letters. When I read them over and over again I can begin to judge how hard my father's demand for $400 hit you. I know that you are poor. I know that you have lost your job. I can feel how much you love me . . .

Perhaps you are right in saying that the church has failed. Certainly you are right when you say that there is a lot of injustice in our young nation. When the new and old bump against each other so suddenly, it can hardly be otherwise. What took so long to happen in Europe is happening so quickly in our country. That is why a useful custom, as the bride-price was in former times, is now being abused—at least so Pastor Walter expressed it. But it is not only the Europeans who are guilty; we also are guilty.

There is a good thing, too, about the bride-price. It shows us girls what we are worth to a man. That's just the way we are. We love the one who has to pay something for us, who has to fight for us, who has to conquer us.

I wrote you at the beginning of this letter: "I love a young man." A man does not only denounce and accuse. A man fights. Accusing God and the whole world doesn't change anything. I respect you only if you fight. And I can love you only if I respect you. That's why I ask you: fight for me. Fight with me for our marriage.

I don't want to leave you alone. I want to fight with you. You are right—many girls do let themselves be sold as goods without showing a will of their own. I do not defend them. But your Cecile wants to be different.

The more we have fought side by side, the more precious our marriage will be. That which just falls into our laps is not worth much. It doesn't bind us together.

I know that God means for us to be together. How I know it, I can't explain. But I know it. Neither can I tell you now how we will find the money, or how my father will change his mind, or how you will find another job. And yet I know, deep down in my heart, that there is a way, so that some day we shall belong to one another.

God doesn't help us by letting money fall into our laps from heaven. But He does go with us step by step through all the difficulties, if we just hold His hand. What we need is not money, but faith—trust in God.

Once more, I love you. But I love the young man François, not the dishrag François.

Your Cecile

B. . . . . , July 22

Dear Cecile,

My husband read to me the letter you wrote to François as you asked him to do. You've hit the nail on the head by this letter—with the sure aim of true love.

First of all I must admit something to you. I never dreamed that a girl your age could write such a letter. Congratulations! I'm so thankful that you've done it and I hope we can get acquainted very soon.

Yes, I know how hard it is to be able to help without hurting. A doctor cannot always heal with a soothing ointment. Often he must use a knife to cut away the infection. In marriage each partner must be the doctor of the other one.

Only the one who is able to heal is also allowed to hurt. This is why love alone can dare to hurt with a good conscience. But love can do it and should do it. For real love is not something sentimental and weak, but something firm and bold.

I was impressed above all that you have already found the connection between respect and love.

In his explanation of the commandment, "You shall not commit adultery," Martin Luther writes as answer to the question, "What does this mean for us?" the following: "We are to fear and love God so that in matters of sex our words and conduct are pure and honorable, and *husband and wife love and respect each other.*"

There is a close connection between respect and love. Still, "respect" has an even deeper meaning than you might think. To respect means to appreciate, to find something worthy of love where no one else can discover it. I believe that a truly loving woman loves her husband even in his weakest hour, in his failure and defeat, even when he lets the leaves hang like a dried-up banana tree. Only the woman who respects her partner in this way really loves him.

Go ahead and send your letter. It is a good letter. God blesses courage and honesty. Don't be afraid. If François sees red, my husband will know how to calm him. Remember here too: "there is no fear in love."

Ingrid T.

E. . . . . , July 27

Sir,

. . . So you have succeeded in getting me to write to you
again . . .

I just received the letter from Cecile which you have
read. It was very clever of you to use her. She knows me
well and knows exactly where I am most easily hurt . . .

But the letter had just the opposite effect from what it
should have had. She doesn't only criticize me; she even
insults me.

And I thought she was an angel! Now the angel has
shown her teeth.

But it's all right. At least I know now where I am. That's
why I'm happy that she wrote me this letter. I have no
more illusions. This disappointment makes it easier for me
to bear my fate.

I possessed the first girl because she said I was no man.
This one I will leave because she says I am no man. You
wrote me once: "True courage here means to flee." So!

What does it say in the Bible—Ephesians 5:22–24? I'll
write it out for you, Mr. Pastor, so that you don't need to
look it up:

Verse 22: "Wives, be subject to your husbands, as to the
Lord."

Verse 23: "For the husband is the head of the wife, as
Christ is the head of the church, his body, and is himself its
Savior."

Verse 24: "As the church is subject to Christ, so let
wives be subject in everything to their husbands."

In *everything*! If she contradicts me now, what would it
be like when we are married? Like all African men, I want
a wife who obeys me—unconditional obedience in *every-*

thing. That's what the Bible says. Just as the Church is subject to Christ, so should wives obey their husbands. That is clear and without question.

I have been warned. Therefore I thank you.

F.

B. . . . . , August 3

Dear François,

This is just the way I thought you would react.

You are very foolish, François. Let me repeat it—very, very foolish.

I read Cecile's letter before she sent it to you. At her request I even read it to my wife. We both wish that many fathers and mothers, young men and girls, would read it, not only in Africa but also in the rest of the world. It's a very unusual letter. We were moved by it.

Your Cecile is no piece of wood, François. Neither is she a baby nor a work-animal without a will of her own. She's not even a servant maid, but instead a very mature girl. I congratulate you on finding such a girl. You have no idea what a great gift it is that such a one loves you.

You wrote to me out of an angry heart after you had read the letter only once. You should never do that. Rather sleep on it for a night, so as to give yourself time to think. Read it again very slowly and quietly. Don't you understand how hard it was for Cecile to write it? That she said these hard things only because she loves you?

Love is not blind; love sees. It sees clearly the weak points and the faults of the other one, but it loves him just the same, including his faults and weaknesses.

You asked me once how someone could know whether he is truly in love. I answered you: by the fact that he is not bothered by the faults of the other one. Of course, he does not love the faults, but he loves the other one with the faults. He feels responsible for the partner.

Now it happens to you that Cecile loves you in this way. But instead of being thankful, you are angry. Or do you think that you have no faults? Perhaps it is impossible to love a person who has no faults.

Be honest. Everything that Cecile said is true. Your trouble is that you give up too quickly.

Yes, I know that criticism hurts, especially that which is true. We are all very sensitive about it. A man is especially sensitive if he is criticized by a woman. This is true in our country as well. But I think African men are over-sensitive on this point. That's because the woman is very seldom looked upon as an equal and one does not accept criticism from inferiors. Here is one reason why so many marriages are so empty and monotonous.

Before he was married, one of my friends wrote to his fiancée about what he expected from his future wife. I'll pick out only a few sentences from the long list he sent her. The first is this:

"She must challenge me to the highest degree by completely honest criticism of me." An un-African sentence, isn't it?

He continued: "When she is disappointed in me, she must not withdraw her confidence."

"She must help me untiringly to overcome my weaknesses."

"She must never pretend, but must tell me honestly when I have hurt her."

Do you understand? What he wanted was not a servant girl, but an equal partner who stands beside him before God. Only with such a partner can you become "one flesh" in the real depths of its meaning—a new, living being. Partnership includes the right to criticize.

And now, Ephesians 5. If we pick out certain verses in the Bible to prove that we are right, then we'd better be careful. Bible verses are not rubber stamps which we can use to certify what we think so that we say, "Just look, even God agrees with me!"

God's word is like a hammer that breaks rocks into pieces, or like a chisel that cuts into us, that may hurt us, in order to form us, change us. God's word challenges us to the highest.

You quoted verses 22–24 because they just suited you. Thanks for copying them for me. But I opened my Bible just the same and read also verses 21 and 25.

Verse 21 emphasizes that submission is mutual. It says: "Be subject to one another out of reverence for Christ."

Then come the verses which you quoted which explain what that means for the man. You left this verse out.

It reads thus: "Husbands, love your wives, as Christ loved the church and gave himself up for her."

That is a tremendous sentence. A whole lifetime is not enough to understand the depth of its meaning.

How did Christ love His Church? He served her. He worked for her and helped her. He healed her, comforted her and cleansed her, even washing her feet—and that was the duty of slaves in Jesus' time. The Church was everything to Christ, and He gave her everything, including His life.

Don't you see how God's word becomes a chisel that cuts and hurts us? It cuts more keenly than any two-edged sword. Christ was not what we men like to be—a big chief or a sheik who wants to be served. He was the slave of His Church. I use this word because it hurts your African ears. Only as the slave of His Church was He her head. So also you are only the head of your wife in the measure in which you are her slave.

Even at that time the Church was not obedient to Him. She left Him in the lurch, and still does up to the present day. You have much to criticize in the Church. So do I. There is so much that is not beautiful in her, if you think about all the tensions and quarrels that go on. But this is the church He loved. He died for her. Through His love He made her lovable.

If the Church obeys Him, then she does not do this because she has to, but because she wants to. Without Him, she cannot live, just as a body cannot live without a head.

Don't you understand that Cecile really wants only one thing: to belong to you just as a body belongs to its head? By criticizing you she wants to reach only one goal: that you will be a head whom she gladly obeys.

That's why she is asking you to fight for her, just as Christ fought for His Church. That's your service to her.

True courage *here* is not to run away, but to become mature.

As soon as possible you should go to Y. and talk to Cecile.

T.

E. . . . . , August 14

Dear Sir,

Again, what a letter! If I didn't know you so well, I should have torn it up. What can I say about it? What a nice sermon!

It's too bad you always look at things with one foot in heaven and the other off the ground. You don't help me towards any practical solution.

The only practical suggestion which you have is in the last line. But even that can't be carried out. How do you think that I could meet Cecile? If I picked her up after school, the news would be all over town right away, and there would be nasty gossip. She lives with her uncle. I wouldn't even dare to show myself there. A park with benches doesn't exist in the whole city. And I haven't a car. If I owned one I would also have money and I could get married.

You don't say a word about money. You talk only about love. But money and love are inseparable in Cameroun. Only those who have money can get married. That is why I need money. I can only get it when I am working. I was a teacher at one of our church schools. The Church dismissed me.

Besides—if Christ is the head of the Church, and the Church is His body, both are one—how is it possible that Christ forgives me and the Church does not?

Then too—I'm entirely on my own. Other young men have a father or family to support them. Here is my situation: My grandfather had three sons: Tonye, Moise, and Otto. Tonye was the oldest. He wasn't a Christian because he had two wives. Moise, the middle son, was a catechist and had only one wife. She bore him four children, two of whom were sons. Otto, the youngest, had only one wife, Martha, who bore him one son, Jacques.

Otto died and Martha became a widow. That is a terrible fate in Africa. When a wife dies, it isn't so bad for a husband. He has lost his property. A property can be replaced if necessary. But a widow is like a property that has lost its owner. She is helpless.

Martha was now a widow with her child Jacques.

Normally, Moise, as the older brother and next in line to Otto, would have had to marry Martha. But that wasn't possible. He was a Christian, and a catechist. He could have only one wife. That is the law of the church. It is hard. The law of our customs and traditions would be more merciful. Because Moise was a catechist, he didn't dare to be merciful.

Moise did take the ten-year-old Jacques into his home and let him go to school. That was all that he could do.

So Martha was pushed on to Tonye. She became his third wife. He hated her from the beginning, and with her he hated Christianity. He neglected her, mistreated her and tormented her. She received neither clothes nor shoes; no hut in which to cook, not even a piece of soap. Nevertheless he had one child by her.

I was that child.

Tonye already had a son by his second wife, who was his favorite wife. He never recognized me as his son.

Only my mother cared for me. I was a dirty, neglected child. I had a skin disease because she had no soap to keep me clean. She could barely clothe me, and I was ashamed to go to school. I ran away and wandered round until I came to the mission station. From there on you know my story.

Do you understand now why I can expect no help from my family? As far as my father goes, I do not exist, especially now that I have become a Christian. My uncle Moise took my half-brother Jacques, and has four children of his own as well. I have only my mother. She has all she can do to live from her garden.

I cannot hope to inherit anything. Even if the favorite son of my father died, both Jacques and the two sons of Moise would come before me.

And now you say, I should go to Cecile. With empty hands? No.

F.

B. . . . . , August 20

Dear François,

Thank you for writing your whole story to me. We have known each other for almost ten years. That is how long it took us to get this far. Why?

Your letter showed me what poor ambassadors for our God we missionaries really are. When you came to me ten years ago you told me that your father was not concerned about either you or your mother. That was true. But I had no idea how much suffering and pain stood behind it. I took you in at our station and didn't ask any more questions.

We always make this mistake. We don't ask any more questions. We don't want to know too much. We are afraid that the burden might crush us. We fear the responsibility.

We missionaries think always we have done enough if we travel to Africa. It's true that we see you daily at the services and in school; but there remains a great distance between us.

We're too lazy really to put ourselves in your shoes, to look at things with your eyes. Instead of this we shut our eyes and simply proclaim the Gospel as a law.

How ashamed Christ must be of His missionaries! As I read your letter, I was ashamed before Christ and within myself. We are so unkind—so lazy in our thinking. Someone who had only one wife becomes a catechist. His brother who has two wives is excluded from the Church. But in your story he actually plays the role of the Good Samaritan.

There just is no solution which applies to everybody. We cannot say: this is right for everyone, and that is wrong for everyone. Love is not lazy. We must take the trouble—the hard labor of love—to search out God's will afresh in each case.

Please forgive me for wanting to keep clear of this work and for not asking you any more questions.

Nevertheless, two things become very clear to me through your letter. Once is this: You should be able to see for yourself now the problems created by polygamy.

You asked me once if it was possible for a man to love several wives at the same time. You see now that it just doesn't work. Either there is no personal relationship between the man and his wives, or he has a favorite wife. In any case, there is always want and emptiness, jealousy and hatred. Even the Bible testifies to that clearly when it describes polygamous relationships.

Just imagine now that your father's favorite son should die. What a fight would take place over the inheritance! Who would be able to unravel the tangle of the rights of the various parties? What a fight there would be, certainly with magic means too, between the brothers, half-brothers, step-brothers and cousins! We would certainly never wish to see it.

The other thing which is clear to me through your letter is this: how God has realized His plan in your life, in spite of all the mix-up of your family, in spite of the guilt of the mission. In spite of everything, He has called you to His kingdom.

God was in everything. In the suffering of your mother, in the lack of love of your father, God was there.

He brought us together. He saved you. He has taken you by the hand and has led you—in spite of your disobedience, in spite of my mistakes—led you to Cecile. What a work of God! *He* was not lazy. Even if we have all failed, He has not failed.

You say my letter was not practical enough. But I can't show you any more than God has shown me for you. Often God does not show us the final solution. He only shows us steps to take.

In Psalm 119 it says: "Thy word is a lamp unto my feet, a light unto my path." God does not promise us headlights that will show us the whole way. He promised only a lamp, and that for our feet. A lamp does not light far ahead, but only a little way.

Your first step is to find work again. I am glad that you thought of that yourself. I suggest you visit Pastor Amos and ask him to re-employ you. I will write to him too and ask him if he will talk to Cecile's father himself. Is that practical enough for you?

And once more: there is no doubt about it, you must talk to Cecile. Don't worry about how you can meet her. A woman thinks with her heart, not with her head. Also in practical things she often has an idea before a man does. Have confidence in Cecile. Love has imagination.

T.

B. . . . . , August 20

Dear Cecile,

François has written to me again. At last he has come out of his hiding place. Your fine letter succeeded in bringing him out.

Now you must be ready. It is possible that he will be waiting for you after school, when it starts again. It will be good for you to plan now where you can go, so that you can talk together in peace . . .

T.

B. . . . . , August 29

Dear Pastor Amos,

I am writing to you today concerning François. You know his story. I baptized him. You confirmed him. Then he became a teacher and I believe he did good work for three years.

Then he had a palaver with a girl. The case was made known among the pupils and he was denounced. Personally, I have the impression that it was a planned trap. He was dismissed because of it, and was forbidden to attend the Lord's Supper for six months.

Then I had a detailed correspondence with him. I'm enclosing copies of some of the letters, so that you have some idea about the case. Finally, it led to a serious conversation in which I was able to help and advise him, and to a confession which went very deep. I cannot tell you more, because the secrets of confession are absolute. I can only testify as his counsellor that he was serious about his repentance, that he accepted the forgiveness of Christ, and that he dared to make a new beginning.

We must stand by his side in this new beginning. You know that there are great temptations to faith after such a complete change around, especially when it is genuine. The devil seems to attack especially hard those who make a decision deep in their hearts. That is why we must both show François brotherly love in his first steps in the new life.

First, I'd like to ask you to allow him to take the Lord's Supper. As far as I can see, the sacrament is only forbidden in the New Testament to those who persist in open sin in spite of many warnings. I cannot find a single case where one who has been repentant and who has confessed his sins has been placed under church discipline.

On the contrary, as his counsellor, I would encourage François to take communion at the next occasion. After his defeat, he will understand it now perhaps for the first time and he will experience it for what it should be: the fellowship of Jesus with sinners.

When we exclude repentant sinners from the Lord's Supper, then it becomes exactly the opposite, a procession of righteous people who proclaim through their taking part that they either have not sinned, or have not been caught at it.

When the prodigal son found his way home again after his life in adultery, his father didn't let him wait for six months in a back room to see whether or not his repentance was genuine. No! He embraced him, accepted him immediately as his son, and ate with him as a sign of forgiveness.

This is now a real problem for François. He writes to me: "Christ has forgiven me, but not the Church. Are these two different things, Jesus Christ and the Church?"

So, do you not think it possible that François might be reemployed as a teacher? That would be a visible sign that not the law but the gospel rules in the Church; not punishment but forgiveness. I have reason for asking this. François has got to know a girl. I think that they really love each other, and are meant for each other. But now the question of the bride-price has come up. This question is a very difficult one for François, for he has no family to support him. You know the situation. The father of the girl is demanding $400 immediately. According to François, this is just a first installment.

Could you not visit this family once? As an African, you would certainly get farther than I could, and you could judge everything much better.

In any case, please give me your opinion and your counsel.

Walter T.

E. . . . . , September 16

Dear Pastor Walter,

We've seen each other.

It was like that first meeting with Cecile. Everything is changed again.

For weeks now I have lived with my mother in a distant little village. For hours I've sat every day in a dimly-lighted hut. My thoughts kept going around in circles—always around the walls. I would stare at the pictures cut out of magazines which I had pasted on the wall as if they could talk to me, give me advice. But always they were silent. At last I couldn't bear to look at them any more. I was trapped in my own prison.

And now the walls have been broken apart. There is freedom everywhere, even though outwardly nothing at all has changed. I'm just as poor as I was before. Only one thing has happened: we have seen each other again.

A friend took me with him in his car. He had to be back the same evening. So I had only two or three hours.

I waited at the entrance of the school. Pupils, both boys and girls, streamed out. Cecile was not among them. Those were terrible minutes.

Finally she came, the very last one. She must have seen me and waited until all the others had gone. She didn't look at me; she just held out her hand. With outstretched arm I touched her fingertips as indifferently as possible, as if we greeted each other in that way every day.

Then she said, as if she had been waiting for me: "There are only two places we can go. We can go into the 'Red Donkey,' or we can go into the Catholic Church. It's always open."

I chose the Catholic Church because I had no money for a restaurant. We had to walk for half an hour to get there.

I went ahead, and she followed me a little distance behind. No one would have guessed that we belonged together.

I would never have thought of going with her to the Catholic Church. It was really open. I asked myself, why are the Protestant Churches always closed?

We entered and sat down on a bench in one of the back rows. We didn't touch each other. We didn't look at each other. Both of us looked straight ahead.

You ask what we talked about. I can't tell you. We hardly talked at all. It was all so completely different from what I had imagined. She said: "I'm glad that you came." I said: "Thank you for your letter."

I really wanted to say something completely different. I wanted to reproach her and to defend myself. But it was as if it were all blown away in her presence.

We were just silent. I don't know how long. Time flew. You understand—we weren't silent out of stubbornness. We were silent together. I could almost say, the silence welded us together.

How easily and how often I used to say to a girl, "I love you," and I wanted to possess her and amuse myself. Now for the first time I should have said it and I couldn't. It was just as if the words were too small, too worn out, to say what the heart was thinking.

We didn't talk, and yet we did talk. Without words both of us knew we loved each other. This certainly worked itself deeper and deeper into our hearts, like a sweet pain, like a great joy.

It was the most beautiful hour of my life. No one should ever take the word "love" in his mouth without having experienced such an hour. It was as if we had known each other always, had always belonged together. It seemed to both of us as if we were one and the same person: she a part of me, I a part of her.

Suddenly I knew for sure: nothing could separate us any longer, no law or custom, no father or mother, no state or church.

Then I remembered that we were in a church. I thought, we are both standing before God, and we are making a promise to each other for life. I took her hand and for a long time our hands lay together, quietly and firmly.

Now I ask you, what is still lacking? Isn't that everything? Are we not married now? When does marriage begin? Does it really begin with the wedding? Doesn't it begin with the engagement, when we promise to each other: "I will belong to you all my life"? We have already made that promise before God. Hasn't our marriage already begun?

I can't even remember now about the farewell. It was as if I was dreaming. She asked me to come again soon, and I said that I was looking for work. Then we left the church one after the other, and went in different directions.

F.

Y. . . . . , September 16

Dear François,

All night I couldn't sleep and I cried. I scolded myself because I didn't talk to you. My heart was so full. I wanted to tell you so much and I couldn't. Now you probably think that I'm indifferent to you, that I don't care.

Please understand that I couldn't speak because I was so happy that you had come. I have no one else but you.

Cecile

E. . . . . , September 18

Dear Cecile,

Don't cry, Cecile, please don't cry. I understand you, understand you deeply. No, you don't need to be afraid. You need never be afraid when I am with you.

It was all my fault. I should have talked; I should have asked you something. But I couldn't either.

It all surprised me so much: how you greeted me, just as a matter of course. How you had prepared everything.

Then you sat beside me as if you were there just for me. That said more to me than all words.

You've cast a spell upon me. . . . I have hope again. Today I helped my mother in the garden instead of staring at the bamboo poles of the roof. She looked at me in amazement.

Your François

B. . . . . , September 19

Dear François,

. . . So you were in the Catholic Church! I told you that Cecile would have a good idea. In Africa it is difficult indeed for a young man to meet a girl! The Church ought to be able to help with this difficulty.

I'm very thankful that you both have experienced this hour, and I can well imagine what feelings were in your hearts.

Your questions are hard to answer. You really have a gift for putting hard questions. They become harder all the time, and I must think about them longer before I can answer them.

When does marriage begin? The Bible says that marriage is a mystery. You cannot explain a mystery. You can only keep penetrating a mystery. You never get to the end of it. The beginning also is a part of the mystery.

You write: "It seemed to both of us as if we were one and the same person." When does a person begin? As far as the outside world is concerned, only from the time of its birth. But life is certainly there before that. When does life begin? Biology says: life begins at the moment of conception.

From that moment on, life is there. A new person has begun. And yet this person cannot be seen. It is in an in-between stage while the mother carries it in her womb. One can only say: a new person is on the way.

That is a picture of engagement and marriage. Your life together has truly begun. Did it really begin in that hour you were together in the church? Wasn't it there already before that? Did it start when you first met on the bus? Or sometime during those weeks of the first ardent correspondence? Who can say? It remains a mystery. From now on this new person, this new living being which you together make up, is on the way.

But this being on the way needs time. This new person must grow slowly just as a child grows in its mother's womb. This growing together slowly will take place during the time of engagement. All that you experience leads to this growth: the beautiful and the difficult; the joy of seeing one another again and the pain of the separation; the speaking and the silence; the writing of a letter and the waiting for an answer; hope and disappointment, yes, even obstacles and sufferings. All that makes the new person which you will become, grow and mature.

But this growth happens in secret. No one knows it, only you two and God—and the few persons in whom you have confided.

So your marriage has begun and still it is not to be seen. It is like the little one in its mother's womb between conception and birth. You are at the in-between stage. Your marriage is on the way.

The wedding day will be the birth-day of your marriage. That is when the new person appears to the world. Then everyone can see it. Then a festival takes place. Then it is made known to everyone.

At the time of engagement you say to one another: "We want to try and see whether we belong together." At the wedding day you say openly in front of everyone: "We have passed the test and it has turned out positively."

Naturally marriage does not come into being through the marriage certificate, any more than a child comes into being through the birth certificate. But still you must not underestimate these things. Marriage is not only a private matter. The official registration also belongs to it. Marriage exists in its fullest state when everybody can see it. At that time it is also protected legally. Luther said once: "A secret marriage is no marriage." That is why the wedding has been celebrated, through all ages and by all people, by a feast.

Please believe me when I say that I can hardly wait to experience this birth-day of your marriage with you. I will gladly do everything that I can, so that it will be soon. That is why I wrote recently to Pastor Amos. But I have not yet received an answer.

T.

O. . . . . , September 20

Dear Pastor Trobisch,

Your letter surprised me in many respects. It was the mission which introduced church discipline to us in Africa, even though it isn't practiced in the European and American churches.

As long as the missionaries put it into practice themselves there were no voices raised against it. Now that we African pastors practice it, you criticize it. Actually we are only doing what you taught us to do.

Would François have come to you and confessed his sin if someone hadn't betrayed him? If he would have done that, if the affair had been known only to him and the girl, then I would say perhaps you are right.

But he was "repentant" only when he was caught. That is why we have to put him to the test in order to see if his repentance is really sincere. Refusing the Lord's Supper to him for six months is just a proving time. It is no sign that he is not forgiven.

This is also a warning to all the others in the congregation. Through such an example they receive power to withstand temptations. If I had not placed François under church discipline, then I would have led many others into temptation. I don't dare to do that. I am responsible for keeping the church pure. In I Corinthians 11:27 it says: "Whoever eats the bread or drinks the cup of the Lord in an unworthy manner will be guilty of profaning the body and blood of the Lord." The sin threatens not only the life of the individual but of the whole congregation.

That is why it is the duty of the Church to punish sin in front of the whole congregation. God also punishes sin in the Bible. David was punished after he confessed adultery with Uriah's wife: his son died. Ananias and Sapphira fell down dead because of a lie (Acts 5:1–11).

I know our African young men better than you do. It is very easy for them to confess something when by doing so they will escape punishment. Your way is very dangerous. If it is so cheap to get forgiveness that one needs only to come to you, and then everything is all right, then the temptation to sin again, rather than to fight against it and turn one's back on it, is very great.

On the other hand, punishment leads to true repentance. If we had not punished François, then probably he would not have repented of his deed.

That is why I can't give him back his job in our school right away. All the teachers and pupils know of his case. If he hadn't been dismissed, that would have undermined the school discipline.

Originally, cases of adultery were rare in African society. They were punished very severely, at times even with death. Missionaries through their preaching have made adultery out to be the chief sin, if not the only sin. Through that they have made it attractive. On the other hand they forbid us to punish it. What shall we do?

I gladly agree to your request and will visit Cecile's family, though I already know with what arguments the father will defend himself. I would like to take François with me. Please ask him to visit me.

Pastor Amos

Y. . . . . , September 22

Dear François,

Your letter comforted me very much. I am happy that you are not angry with me. I wanted to write to you before. But we had so much homework to do.

I have good news for you. My friend Bertha has an uncle who works in the Ministry of Education. She says he would like to give you a job as a teacher on one of the public schools in Y.

Please accept this offer. Then you can earn money and we can see each other every day.

Your Cecile

E. . . . . , September 24

Dear Pastor,

Thank you for your letter. I had to think it over for a long time. The comparison between the time of engagement and the time of pregnancy is interesting. But when a child is conceived, it is easy to work out roughly what the date of its birth will be. I can't work out when we may be able to be married. That is what makes the waiting so difficult.

Your letter came in the same mail with one from Cecile. I'm enclosing it. What do you say about it? Is it possible for me as a Christian to teach in a public school?

Do you think it is good for us both to be in the same city? I long for it. And yet I know already I would miss Cecile's letters.

François

B. . . . . , September 27

Dear François,

. . . Of course you can work in a public school as a Christian. If the Church could have given you a job, then it
would have been right to take it. But Pastor Amos wrote
to me that under the present circumstances it would be
impossible. We must try to see his reasons. We must also
understand that he has reached his decision only after
much thought and prayer.

For you that means the way is free. God leads us step by
step, just as He promises us only our daily bread, and not
our whole livelihood.

My advice is this: accept the position in Y. Perhaps your
testimony can be even more effective when you live
among non-Christians. Be on the alert, and keep your eyes
open.

Also, for the sake of your future marriage, it is good to
see each other often. I wrote to you before that your engagement time should be a time of preparation. Your life
together has begun, but at present it is still being tested.
Not that you have to test Cecile, nor she you. But you both
seek together to know whether you can become one in
spirit before God.

For that purpose letters are often very helpful, because
you can write many things which are hard to say in person.
But you cannot really get to know each other just through
letters. You must meet one another in different situations,
in good moods and bad. You need to talk together so that
you can get to know each other fully.

Being silent is part of the conversation. You have experienced that already. But it is only a part. Now you must
also find words. You must find out if you can talk to each

other and also if you can listen to each other. A marriage without plenty of talk is like a plant without sap. One day it will dry up.

It isn't necessary for you always to have the same opinion. But you must love each other so much that you will value each other's opinions.

One thing will become more difficult if you see each other every day and that is to draw a limit and to keep within it, withstand temptation. Imagine that you were a father of a fifteen-year-old daughter. Everything that you would not wish to be done to your daughter, you should not do to Cecile. I remind you again of all that I told you at the beginning of the year about becoming a man.

One more thing. Pastor Amos wrote to me that he will visit Cecile's father and that he would like you to go with him. On your way to Y. please stop at the pastor's house and fix a date. I will think about you especially on that day.

T.

B. . . . . , September 28

Dear Pastor Amos,

Your letter, dear Brother Amos, is very matter-of-fact, almost cold. That is how I know that my last letter must have hit you very hard, and I can feel how difficult it was for you to answer me at all.

Thank you all the more for writing to me, and especially for writing so frankly and honestly.

Yes, we missionaries have made mistakes. We must regret many things we have done. I've written the same thing to François, in whose life story the mission is not without blame.

The miracle is that, in spite of our mistakes, God has built a church. To Him alone be the glory!

I would not defend myself, if it were for my sake. But it is for the sake of François and for so many others who are in his position. For their sakes we must seek to find what is the will of God. Please believe me, this was why I asked certain questions.

Is there really any human way by which we can determine the sincerity of repentance? Is it proof of true repentance if one lets go of a certain sin for a certain time? Is it not God alone who can see into the heart?

You quote I Corinthians 11. There it says: "Let a man examine himself." (Verse 28) Isn't that exactly the opposite of what we practice in the African churches, where it is the pastor and elders of a congregation who examine the members? And even if that were commanded, why should not the pastors and missionaries also be examined?

Who is "worthy" at all? Am I? Are you? If only the worthy ones were permitted to go to Communion, who would dare to go? Only those who are conscious of their unworthiness are really worthy to attend.

It is this truth which François has discovered and now knows more deeply and more clearly than ever. That is why he looks for and needs the fellowship of Jesus. As men then, do we dare to stand between him and his Lord? Do we dare to withhold from him that which Christ wishes to give him?

Yes, I admit: God does punish. But in all the examples which you give it is always God who punishes, not men, not the church.

Dear Brother Amos: you have put a serious question before us pastors. Is it not a lack of faith which stands behind church discipline?

And now one last question: do you really think that it is so simple and easy to confess your sins? That's what those who have never done it often say. For me it was the hardest step that I ever took. Also for François. He had a hard battle with himself. I can testify to that. A counsellor can feel it. It was costly grace for him—grace which cost Christ His life. And still the paradox remains: This costly grace is offered to us absolutely free.

I can understand what you write about school discipline. Certainly a school is not a church. I don't think it would be good for François to go back to the same school. But maybe there is another solution.

I have already written to François that he should look you up. Thank you very much for your readiness to go with him to Cecile's father. May God give you much wisdom for this visit. I will think about you specially on that day.

Walter T.

Y. . . . . , October 17

Dear Pastor,

I have now been in Y. for two weeks. No, almost three weeks. How the time flies.

On the way here I visited Pastor Amos. He was very friendly to me: I was really surprised. Tomorrow we will go together to Cecile's father. My half-brother Jacques will come with us as the representative of our family. So it will be an official visit.

But before I go there I want to send you a few lines. Cecile has actually succeeded in finding work for me. Every morning when I enter school I am grateful to Cecile. But I am still more grateful each evening when I can see her.

Cecile is a genius; she has ideas. Recently she has borrowed two bicycles. With these we can ride out every day into the bush after school is over until it gets dark. Then she has to go home to her uncle.

Yes, and now we are "discovering" each other, as you would express it. Each day is full of new discoveries. A girl is certainly unknown territory. Now for the first time I see how blind I was when I considered a girl as I would a toothbrush—something which one uses. And I wanted to "use" one in order to know how a "woman" is—oh!

Now I want to get to know only one girl—and that girl is called Cecile. It is as if all the others no longer exist. In her I get to know all girls, all women . . .

I let her ride ahead of me so that I can see her. She has her hair fastened up on her head, so I can see her long slender neck. I dreamt of it the other night. When we go up a hill she has to exert herself and pushes harder on the pedals. Then her beautiful neck moves in rhythm with her body. I could watch her doing this for hours.

Then we get off our bicycles and sit in the grass. There's hardly a topic that we haven't already talked about. She has her own opinion about everything. I didn't know that a girl could think, let alone have her own opinions.

As fascinating to me as what she says is the way she says it. I listen then to the sound of her voice, watch her hands and her eyes.

In those moments I would like to touch her. You told me once: "Keep your caresses for your fiancée." But Cecile now is my fiancée. How far do I dare to go? You advised me to keep within the limit. But what is the limit?

Oh, I'll tell you right away: we kiss. That far it always goes. Not right away. At first we both feel a little strange. Each time we have to get reacquainted. But while we talk, our hands look for each other. I can tell that she is waiting until I take hold of her hand, her arm. She is even pleased when I lean her head on my shoulder. She smiles a little, is very quiet, as if she just tolerates it. Then comes the kiss.

I must confide something else to you. When I kiss her, then the desire rises within me to possess her completely. I can't put it down.

If you had not reminded me of my own daughter on some future day; if Cecile had not written to me once: "I loved you even more because in that first night you didn't come to me," I don't know what might have happened by this time.

When I dedicated myself to Christ that night at your home, I thought that I was set free. You said then, "Christ is not a nothing. He is a power. Through His power you can overcome."

At first it seemed that way. But now the desire is stronger than ever. My faith doesn't help me. Christ doesn't hear my prayers. They fall into emptiness. The desire is stronger than Christ. Why doesn't Christ help me, do something to me, so that I can be finished with this desire, this craving to possess a girl—once and for all?

The experience of love destroys my faith. Or must one who believes flee from love?

I'm afraid. Afraid of myself. Afraid of the animal which sleeps within me.

Do you understand?

Tomorrow I am going on a trip. When I return after two or three days, there must be a letter from you. Otherwise there might be a disaster.

François

B. . . . . , October 18

Dear François,

It is almost midnight. But I want to answer your letter right away.

You write that Christ hasn't heard your prayer. I ask you, what did you pray for? That He would deliver you from being a man? What do you want? To be without sex? To have no more desire at all?

What you speak of is not possible. All that one does, one does either as a man or woman. Your sexuality is in your waking and sleeping. It is present with you when you work and when you pray. In your holiest feelings and in your purest prayers it is there.

If you believe in Christ, then you know that your body has become the temple of the Holy Spirit. If you pray for the mutilation of the temple, then Christ will not hear you. Christ wants to make you capable of living with your manhood.

Must the one who believes flee from love? I know there are many Christians who withdraw themselves and who turn their backs on it. They avoid the opposite sex and think by doing so that they are especially mature and redeemed Christians.

They fool themselves. He who believes does not flee.

Christ did not evade this issue. He came into this world. He was a young man. He came into touch with women's hands, women's kisses, women's tears.

He came to the bedside of a sick woman. He took a young girl by the hand. A woman touched His robe. Two women who loved Him are called by their names, Mary and Martha. He spoke with women alone, once at the well and another time writing in the sand. The sinner who kissed His feet was a woman of bad reputation. Those in the room were shocked. Yet He defended her. He moved among people in a free and natural way.

He is the one who has overcome because He lived the life of a human being. To overcome means to be on the way to mastery. He will lead you to that goal, not to flight.

You can't run away from your manhood: it belongs to you; it is a part of yourself.

Let me tell you a story:

Once upon a time there was a tiger. He was captured and put in a cage. The keeper's task was to feed him and guard him.

But the keeper wanted to make the tiger his friend. He always spoke to him in a friendly voice whenever he came to his cage. The tiger, however, always looked at him with hostility in his green glowing eyes. He followed every movement of the keeper, ready to spring on him.

The keeper was afraid of the tiger and asked God to tame him.

One evening, when the keeper had already gone to bed, a little girl lost in the vicinity of the tiger's cage and came too near to the iron bars. The tiger reached out with his claws. There was a blow, a scream. When the keeper arrived he found dismembered human flesh and blood.

Then the keeper knew that God had not tamed the tiger. His fear grew. He drove the tiger into a dark hole where no one could come close to him. Now the tiger roared day and night. The terrible sound disturbed the keeper so that he could no longer sleep. It reminded him of his guilt. Always in his dreams he saw the torn body of the little girl. Then he cried out in his misery. He prayed to God that the tiger might die.

God answered him, but the answer was different from what the keeper had expected. God said, "let the tiger into your house, into the rooms where you live, even into your most beautiful room."

The keeper had no fear of death. He would rather die than go on hearing the roar of the tiger. So he obeyed. He opened the door of the cage and prayed: "Thy will be done."

The tiger came out and stood still. They looked into each other's eyes for a long time. As soon as the tiger noticed that the keeper had no fear and that he breathed quietly, he lay down at his feet.

That is the way it began. But at night the tiger would begin to roar again, and the keeper would be afraid. So he had to let the tiger come into his house and face him. Again he had to look the tiger directly in the eye. Again and again. Every morning.

He never had the tiger completely in his power "once and for all." Again and again he had to overcome him. Every day brought the same test of courage.

After some years the two became good friends. The keeper could touch the tiger, even put his hand between his jaws. But he never dared to take his eyes off the tiger. When they looked at each other they recognized each other and were glad that they belonged together and that each was necessary to the other.

François, you have to learn to live with the tiger, courageously, eye to eye. For that purpose Christ will set you free.

If you believe in Him, then you can dare to be tender to each other. There are Christians who think that God is especially pleased with them if they deny themselves this. But that is nonsense. Only he who truly believes can also really love.

How far do I dare to go? How far? As far as you can. Put your hand in the jaws of the tiger if you can.

But don't overestimate your strength and don't skip over any of the steps. You must learn to feel which caresses are right for the particular occasion. Please don't think, just because many do it so quickly and easily, that kissing is not an art.

Never take your eye off the tiger. He is awake and prowling. He follows every movement, knows every weakness.

François, I am sending you along a dangerous road. But I am glad you tell me everything. I don't want you to be evasive. Once more: He who believes does not flee.

I will give this letter tomorrow morning—no, this morning, because it was midnight long ago—to one of my friends who is going to Y., so that it will reach you quickly.

T.

O. . . . . , October 23

Dear Brother Walter,

I want to tell you about our visit to Cecile's father.

But first, thank you for your letter of September 19. It did me a lot of good to hear from the mouth of a white man, even that of a missionary, that the whites are not without fault.

Your statement, that God can build the Church even in spite of us when we fail, has comforted me greatly.

As far as church discipline is concerned the question for me is always this: is there forgiveness without punishment?

Even the heathen believe that God punishes when His commandments are broken.

Then the missionaries came and said: God does not punish, rather God forgives. The result is that wherever Christianity has advanced, indiscipline breaks out. The heathen fear God, the Christians don't. They say: God doesn't punish, God forgives. So I don't risk anything if I sin.

What are we able to do then? I don't dare to act as you suggest. Perhaps I lack faith. Perhaps you Europeans have more faith than we do. Do your congregations really live more obediently than our congregations? Or do you just shut your eyes because you don't want to see sin?

For us Africans, when sin happens, it hurts not only the individual but the whole community. In this way I believe we are closer to the thinking of the Bible than you are. You didn't go into this point. This is also the vital point in the marriage palaver about Cecile. For her father, the marriage of his daughter is not only an affair between Cecile and François. It concerns the whole family. It isn't he who sets the bride-price. His brothers and above all the brothers and father of Cecile's mother set the price for him.

He has nothing personal against François. He thinks he is a decent and honest young man. But this is how Cecile's father is placed.

His first wife bore him no child. He felt however that he must have a son. He was convinced that he owed his father this debt: to pass on the life which he received from him. Otherwise his own life would not make sense.

So he took a second wife. She bore him Cecile and then shortly after that three sons.

It is true that he is certainly not one of the poorest in his village. He is a very industrious man who has a large cocoa plantation. But in spite of that, up till now he has only been able to pay half of the bride-price for Cecile's mother. The other half has to come out of the bride-price for Cecile.

Besides that he has three sons whom he wishes to send to school. The cost of tuition rises from year to year. And one day these three sons will want to marry also. But he has only one daughter for these three sons.

He is not just wanting to be rich, nor is he lazy; rather he is very conscious of his responsibility. Cecile's uncles on her mother's side also keep their eyes on him.

We talked together quietly. He feels that a woman is more obedient to her husband if he has paid something for her. Otherwise it would be easy for her to run away whenever there was a dispute, and say: "I don't belong to you, because you paid nothing for me." Also the husband, he says, remains more faithful to his wife if she has cost him something. In earlier times the bride-price was paid in cattle. If the marriage broke up, the cattle would have to be given back. So that helped to keep marriage together.

By introducing money into the country the Europeans have destroyed this custom—that's what Cecile's father thinks. Behind it is also a reproach against me, because I have let myself become like a European. He doesn't say it outright, but I know it.

For him the bride-price is an honorable African custom through which the son-in-law shows the bride's father his gratitude and proves to him at the same time that he is capable of taking care of a wife.

There is another reason for the large amount of money he asks. My guess is that he is thinking about taking a third wife. He didn't say that to me, but I suspect it. The birth of the three sons, coming so quickly after each other, has made Cecile's mother very weak. Polygamy makes it possible to avoid that situation. The Church says: polygamy is sin; but it does not tell us how to space the children.

We ask ourselves sometimes how the missionaries solve this problem. But they always keep silent on this subject.

Now you can understand how it looks from the other side. What should I do? I don't know myself how I should be able to pay for the education of my sons if I gave away my daughter without a bride-price. Cecile's father doesn't understand what love is. How shall I explain that to him?

You will probably be disappointed and think that I as an African could have done more than I did. That may be true. He certainly told me more than he would have told you. But there are also disadvantages.

Cecile's father and I—we are from the same clan. So we are distantly related. That hinders me, because I am too involved myself. In such a case perhaps you as a European could do more than I. You are neutral. You come from the outside. You could try . . .

I was very happy about François. He was modest and didn't try to push himself forward. But he will have to wait until he has more money. I don't see any other solution.

Pastor Amos

B. . . . . , October 26

Dear Cecile,

François will have told you how the visit to your father turned out. I received a detailed letter about it from Pastor Amos.

Cecile, please don't lose courage. God is with us, even in the darkness. True faith begins there, where one doesn't see at all. When all else forsakes us, all human hope, all possibility of a solution, then there is only one thing left for us to do; to let ourselves fall into God's arms. God is never closer to us than in such moments. "Fear not, *only* believe," the Bible commands. We are only fully in God's hands when we have Him alone.

"*Only believe!*" That is something which must be learned. You and François must learn it together now. Nothing can prepare you better for your future marriage. That is why God sends you now into this darkness, takes away all supports upon which you could lean. So that you can learn and practice together to put your confidence in God *alone.*

How can you learn it? First of all: let God speak to you and listen to Him. When you are together, then open up your Bibles and read a portion together. Talk about it— what He says to you. Allow yourselves to be comforted, counselled and guided by God.

Then fold your hands together and spread out your worries before God. He knows the way. He will take you by the hand and lead you. He has brought you together. He will hinder the attempt of people to separate you. Believe that with all your hearts.

Don't be embarrassed to pray in front of one another. You will have to overcome this feeling of embarrassment. Now is your chance to learn it. Now you will see if you can talk about everything—also about your faith. A common faith is the most solid foundation for a marriage. If you build your house on this rock, then no storm can destroy it.

I talked for a long time yesterday with Ingrid about what could be done in your case.

First of all, we suggest that you write a letter of thanks to Pastor Amos. He is a good shepherd. It is touching that the old man undertook such a long and difficult trip. We respect him greatly.

And now we have a favor to ask of you, Cecile. That is the reason I write to you, although the letter is meant for both of you.

From your letter of July 19, written to François, it was clear that God has given you the gift of writing good letters. Now we ask you: would you consider writing your father a letter? We know that is something very unusual for an African girl. Perhaps that is why it could be effective.

Two things seem hopeful to us in Pastor Amos's account. In one place he writes about your father: "He has nothing personal against François." And then: "He doesn't understand what love is."

Try, Cecile, to explain to your father what your love for François is—to give him a feeling of it. We often reproach fathers because they do not talk to their daughters. Perhaps it is rather the opposite: the daughters do not speak to their fathers. They do not tell them what they feel, what they suffer and what they hope.

Write this letter in your mother tongue. Write that you love your father, that you understand him, and that you don't want to leave him in the lurch.

Give him some practical suggestions. You will think of something. Of course François must be in accord with such suggestions. In that way you can try out something else: whether or not you can plan your finances together.

It is not enough during the time of your engagement just to see whether you understand each other, whether you can be tender to each other, whether you can believe and pray together. You must also see if you have the same attitude towards money, so that you can decide together about what you spend. A wife should know how much her husband earns, and you must be in agreement as to how you will spend your money.

Your attitude towards money is much more important than how much money you have.

And still one other thing, Cecile, which I tell you in confidence. At the beginning of the year, even before he met you, I wrote to François, "You are responsible before God for the girl."

Now I write the same thing to you. You, a girl, determine how far François can go. No young man can go further than the girl allows. Don't have any false pity. Be a queen. You love a young man. Make him a mature young man.

T.

Y. . . . . , November 1

Dear Pastor and Madame,

Thank you very much for your letter. I read it to François and we were both very moved to know you can put yourselves in our situation, that you feel exactly as we feel and that you want to comfort us.

We didn't know that God cared so much about us, that faith had anything to do with engagement. Without faith, we would have to give up now. But just because we do not know what the future holds, we feel even more closely bound together.

We have tried for the first time to read the Bible together. At first it seemed very strange. But then it was wholesome. It helps us if we are not only tender to one another, but if we are doing something else together. But we haven't prayed together yet. I'm ashamed to pray aloud in front of François.

I have tried to write to my father, but it just doesn't work. I can't tell you how hard it is for me. As a European I don't think you can understand it. It is as if there is a wall which separates me from my father.

Our fathers do not like to hear their daughters speak to them. They are afraid they will lose their authority. They think we do not respect them and they are offended.

I know that you meant your suggestion well. I have begun a letter and will try to continue it. Every line is a battle. It is so hard to put into words what I feel.

But even if I write it, I know I will never have the courage to send the letter.

Cecile

Y. . . . . , November 7

Dear Pastor Walter,

I am glad that your letter was here when I got back from that fruitless trip to Cecile's father.

I thought: what happens to all those who don't have anyone to whom they can write a letter, no one who answers them . . . ?

The story about the tiger is not bad. It shows me that neither those who put the tiger in a cage nor those who let him free are doing the right thing. The ones who follow the world are just as cowardly as those who are super-pious. We mustn't give up the fight. It is not the fault of the tiger if we fall. It is up to me whether the tiger is my enemy or my friend. I have understood all that.

But there is still one question unanswered. What does it mean: "to put your hand in the tiger's jaws"? Does that mean I can go to the end if I am master of myself, quiet and "don't skip any of the steps," as you say? Does this mean that we can become united bodily?

I asked you this question before. Then it was about a girl I didn't care about, I didn't wish to marry, and whom I hardly knew. Do you remember?

I said then that I wanted to prepare myself for marriage. And you answered: on the contrary! You are learning habits which will disturb your marriage later on.

I said I had to take a girl now and then in order not to be ill. You answered again: on the contrary. You risk your health by doing that.

I said I wanted to prove that I was a man. You answered the third time: on the contrary, you are a dishrag.

You convinced me then. But you didn't go into one argument: that of true love!

What if one wishes to be united out of love? If it only concerned some girl on the streets, I grant you are right. But with one's fiancée? With the girl that you love, with whom you feel completely one, to whom you have made a promise for life? Why should one stop there just with caresses, when you can say, in the deepest sense of the word, that you belong together?

You said that you can never try out being with just any girl in this intimate way. I agree. But can't you try it out with your own fiancée? If engagement time is supposed to be a trial time, why shouldn't you try out *that* also? Would you say that also is "adultery," if an engaged couple should give themselves completely to each other?

I heard a pastor say once: "Marriage is a garden in which everything is allowed. Outside of the garden, everything is forbidden." Yes, and then suddenly on my wedding day, I am expected to be a perfect husband? How can you imagine that would be possible?

Please understand me rightly: I am not asking the right to spend the night with just any girl off the street. I'm talking about Cecile, whom I am going to marry.

Do we really need first a note of permission from the registrar's office or from the church in order to be united physically? Inwardly we feel already as much man and wife as we would after the wedding.

Sometimes I have the impression that Cecile waits secretly for the moment when she can belong to me completely. I have a friend who had already paid half the bride-price. But he didn't wish to sleep with his fiancée before the wedding. One day he received the money back from the girl's family. The family was afraid that he was impotent. I wonder sometimes whether Cecile suspects this when I do not take her. Perhaps she even thinks that I don't really love her?

Recently she stretched out in the grass. Just lay there.
Gazing up into the sky. Completely innocent. Her dress
was tight across her breasts, and her knees were uncov-
ered. I just couldn't hold back any longer, and I took her
in my arms with all my strength. But she broke away from
me and ran to the place where our bicycles were standing.
We didn't say a word all the way home, nor did we talk
about it the next day.

How long can this continue? How long must we keep
ourselves from each other? If only the end were in sight!
But we have no hope that in the next four, five or even ten
years someone will give us a license.

Shall we run away? Where to?

François

B. . . . . , November 11

Dear François,

A Christian is one who can wait. Someone gave this to me as a word of advice. I pass it on to you. Wait for the complete union. By not waiting you will gain nothing and you will lose much. I will put what you would lose into three words: freedom, joy and beauty.

You would lose freedom.

Let me tell you about another couple I know. They too thought that they loved each other and that they felt inwardly already as man and wife. But after six months they noticed that they had made a mistake. They talked openly about their feelings and agreed mutually to break their engagement. It all happened very peacefully. No scars remained.

If they had given themselves to each other completely, that would not have been possible. I know that your feeling for Cecile is so much deeper that it could not be compared to your feeling for that girl at the beginning of the year. And that is just the reason why I advise you to wait. The deeper your feeling is for each other, the more lasting would be the wounds in case of a separation.

I have heard men who have been married for years say to their wives: "I knew before the wedding that I had made a mistake. But we had already gone so far that I didn't have the courage to break it off. Now I have to pay the price for my mistake."

I am glad to read in your letters how strong and true and overpowering is the love you are experiencing. Nevertheless feelings can deceive you. It takes a long time before you can really decide whether you sense something lasting. A recent survey in America has shown that in most of the happy marriages the partners have known each other for several years, and that they were engaged several months before their marriage.

A test is only genuine if it could turn out to be negative. The time of engagement is a time of testing only if there is the possibility of breaking the engagement. Breaking an engagement is an evil. It is painful. No one wishes it. But in comparison to a later divorce, it is certainly the lesser evil.

I will use the picture of a birth again in order to make clearer what the engagement means. If I compare marriage with a child which is ready to be born, then the time of engagement is the time before birth. A broken engagement would be then—using this picture—like a miscarriage, which is what happens when a child is not able to live. In the moment, however, that you come together, you reach a stage where a miscarriage becomes almost impossible. Then there is no turning back and a separation would be like the murder of a child.

So you would lose your freedom. But even more: You would spoil the joy which the growing, maturing and waiting brings with it. Having sexual relations now before marriage reminds me of the child who, out of sheer impatience, opened his Christmas presents on the twenty-second of December. A married woman, talking about her experience before marriage, put it once this way: "Everything went along fine for a while. But then there came an unexpected pregnancy. Plans had to be changed quickly and excuses had to be made. The wedding was celebrated hurriedly. Our married life began without romance and without dignity. It didn't pay."

A premature birth endangers the life of the child. Of course, many children survive a premature birth. But never without difficulty.

When Cecile ran away from your sudden embrace, she just reacted naturally and without long reflection. Her healthy, unspoiled instinct protected her. She felt that the time was not yet ripe, that your happiness would be put in danger through this step. Actually your harmony was also broken and you didn't speak to each other any more that day.

I do not really believe that Cecile doubts your love when you restrain yourself. It is much more possible that her love grows. Your being together is still in a hidden stage. It is right also at this stage that you have not completely revealed or unveiled yourselves to each other. On your wedding day a piece of undiscovered land should still lie before you.

Of course the sexual side of your marriage is very important. You know already that you are not impotent, and Cecile knows it too. If there were any doubts, then a doctor could confirm it. That is no reason for wounding Cecile's feelings nor for risking your happiness.

Sexual harmony cannot be tried out. Even an engaged couple cannot determine it reliably before the wedding. There are two conditions necessary and both of these can be found only after the wedding: unlimited time and being completely free from fear.

If Cecile has to say to herself: "Today between five and six P.M. I must meet François. Then it must happen. Then I must be ready. Then it must succeed—otherwise he will leave me."—I can tell you now with certainty: these thoughts will check her and lame her, so that both of you will be disappointed.

Suppose you tried it out and it turned out negatively? Suppose it didn't work as you thought it should. Would you then say: we shall have to break our engagement? You don't believe that. Your love is not that superficial. It is already too deep. Why then do you want to experiment?

No one expects you to be a perfect married couple on your wedding day. There is no such thing as a perfect married couple. There is only a mutual growing towards perfection. Often it takes years before man and wife are really adjusted to each other. The unlimited time which you need for growth you will find only in marriage. All that you can do before marriage is to protect yourself from experiencing or learning things which will hinder you from growing.

You can't have your cake and eat it too. The magic and beauty of the engagement period lies in the fact that there still remains one last secret, there is still a room which will only be entered when the hour has come.

Just imagine that your father wants to surprise you with a bicycle for Christmas. He hides it carefully. But you take it secretly out of the hiding place and try it out. Then on Christmas Day you have to act as if you are surprised and joyful, but the holiday is colorless and empty.

Your wedding day and your first night will become more beautiful if you have waited. Not until that night will you understand me fully. The wedding is not only a formality. If you have testified in public, before God and men: "We belong together," then the experience will be much deeper and it will have a much fuller meaning when you give yourselves to each other completely.

We tell our children in Europe a fairy tale: A king's daughter was put under a magic spell by a witch, and she had to sleep for a hundred years until a prince would awaken her with a kiss. In order to protect the princess, the king planted a hedge of thorns which grew up all around the castle. All the princes who tried to break their way in before the one hundred years were up were caught in this hedge and died. But for the prince who could wait, the thorns yielded and the way was free.

I can only put you into the hands of your heavenly Father. He will give you something beautiful. Let me say it again: A Christian is one who can wait.

You won't be able to reach me by letter during these next few weeks. I have to make a trip to the North. But I hope to be back before Christmas.

T.

Y. . . . . , November 12

Dear Madame Ingrid,

I was so surprised when François introduced me to you yesterday after the service that I couldn't say anything. I'm sorry that you had to leave so quickly and that your husband wasn't with you. How much I would like to get to know him also!

I wanted to write to you before. But now that we've seen each other it will be easier for me. Strange, but I just can't write to my father. I've already made many notes of what I want to tell him, I've begun the letter, but again and again I've had to stop. A letter just won't come out of it all.

Still, I have the feeling that you will understand me. You probably think that I am very happy, and I am. Just the same my heart is often heavy. I have doubts, and I'm afraid.

I have doubts about whether François really loves me. He never tells me that he does. He often asks me if I love him, and he can't hear my answer often enough. But he never says that he loves me. Then doubts arise in my heart. I can only love him if I can answer to his love. He seems to think it isn't necessary to tell me that he loves me, and why he loves me. How can I answer him then? He makes me so uncertain. How can you test love?

Your husband has written to François the story about the princess. I wonder what the prince did after he had awakened the princess. Was he not very careful, very tender, so that she wouldn't be afraid? Did he not tell her how much he loved her, and why?

Just lately we had a quarrel. It was about something very trivial and ridiculous. I had a flat tire on one of our daily bicycle rides. I had a repair kit and François mended the tire. That made him bad-tempered—and me too—because of the time we had lost. When he had finished, we discovered that I had left the pump at home. I always take it off, to prevent it being stolen. Then he started to scold me, and said it just proved that girls have no intelligence. I was hurt because he was so rude, and out of stubbornness I didn't say a single word while we pushed our bicycles home. It was nothing serious at all. The next day we made it up again. But I ask myself—if we have quarrels already, what will it be like later on?

And then I'm afraid. I would like to be sure whether I can bear a child or not. I'm afraid that François will divorce me if I am barren. Or that he will take a second wife, like my father. Is there any justification for marriage if there is no child?

Then there is still another problem. Lately I received the enclosed letter from a certain Monsieur Henri. He is a brother of the uncle of my friend Bertha who helped François to get his job as a teacher in Y. This Monsieur Henri works in the Ministry of Finance and has a good position. He even wanted to pick me up in his car.

Of course I refused him. What shall I do if he invites me again? I don't want to be rude.

Please answer me!

Cecile

Y. . . . . , November 9
Ministry of Finance

Dear Mademoiselle Cecile,

Your friend Bertha has told me about you. I would like to make your worthy acquaintance, and shall be honored to wait for you in my car tomorrow at five P.M. outside your school entrance.

Monsieur Henri

B. . . . . , November 18

Dear Cecile,

How well I understand you, my sister! I could show you letters from the time of my engagement in which I expressed the same anxieties and doubts.

But we also do not make it easy for the men, Cecile. On the one hand we want a man to be strong, wise and unsentimental. On the other hand we want him to be full of feeling, to be tender and to need us. What man can combine the answer to both of these wishes in a single person?

I will try to write directly to François. Don't ask him about the letter if he does not show it to you himself. For you there is only one way—you must tell him frankly and honestly when something is wrong, when you are hurt. As long as you can do that, then there is no danger to your marriage.

One thing more: you cannot prove or measure the quantity of love before marriage. It is not true that marriage grows only out of love. The opposite is also true: love grows out of marriage, sometimes very slowly. In the Old Testament story of Isaac and Rebecca it says: "Then Isaac brought Rebecca into the tent, and took her, and she became his wife; and he loved her" (Genesis 24). They married without having seen each other beforehand. The falling in love came afterwards.

Most of the marriages that you see around you were begun without any great personal love experience. Often the girls weren't even asked. You know yourself that they are not all unhappy. Often love has grown after the wedding as a fruit of the marriage.

A man from India once said to a European: "You marry the girl that you love. We love the woman that we have married!" Another Indian put it even more drastically: "We put cold soup on the fire, and it becomes slowly warm. You put hot soup into a cold plate, and it becomes slowly cold." You'll have to decide yourself on which side you Africans belong.

I am writing in this way so that you will not overestimate the love experience. It is certainly important. But love will become fully mature only in the atmosphere of marriage.

It is not only good, it is even necessary that you have some disagreements. My husband even hesitates to marry a couple who have not yet had a quarrel! What counts is not that you never quarrel, but that you are able to make up after a quarrel. That is an art which can and must be learned before marriage. As long as you are able to forgive each other you don't need to be worried about the future of your marriage.

The one who is not ready to be the first to apologize after a quarrel should not marry; and the one who has no humor had also better not marry. It is wonderfully wholesome if you can laugh about yourselves after a quarrel.

When you ran away from François, it was the thorn hedge in you which reacted—the thorn hedge which protects the sleeping princess. Many girls who give themselves too early never become mature. That is why it says three times in the Old Testament book, *The Song of Solomon* "I adjure you . . . that you stir not up nor awaken love until it please." This entreaty stands as if it were written in flames above the door of marriage.

Perhaps the waiting will be easier if you don't see each other daily. Then each meeting will be more significant. There are no rules about this. You must find out what is best for the two of you.

How well I understand your wish—your heart's desire for the happiness of motherhood! But the most frequent

cause of sterility is venereal disease. That is why virgins
have every chance of becoming mothers. But you can't be
sure about God's will in this matter until you are married;
then you receive the knowledge that you will become a
mother as a gift from God. There is no other way.

But do not think that if you have a pregnancy before
marriage it can be compared with the deep happiness of
motherhood! True, one problem is solved: you know that
you can conceive a child. But how many new problems
arise. There is no home in which the little one can be
born, no father who can carry the child on his arm. There
will even be a dispute about whom the child belongs to as
long as the father has paid no bride-price. You will have to
leave school and be made fun of and criticized by your
teachers and classmates. For the certainty that you gain,
you must exchange feelings of shame and guilt, self-re-
proach and the loss of self-respect. It doesn't pay. The
price is too high.

Or do you have the secret desire, through a pregnancy,
to force your father to consent to the wedding? Please,
please, I beg of you, don't do that! Don't lower your child
to be a means by which you can ready your own goal. God
has another solution if you can wait.

Give all your anxieties about motherhood to God. Even
if you should have no child, that is no ground for a divorce. Your husband also has no right to take a second
wife if your marriage has been registered as a monoga-
mous marriage.

A Christian marriage has meaning and purpose even if
God should give no children to the couple. The Bible
speaks about marriage only in a very few places. So it is all
the more striking that the same verse is quoted four times:
"Therefore a man leaves his father and his mother and
cleaves to his wife, and they become one flesh." (Genesis

2:24; Matthew 19:15; Mark 10:7, Ephesians 5:31). Notice how in this key verse, repeated four times, there is no word about children. According to the Bible, children are an added blessing of God. But they are not the only reason for marriage. The love of the two partners for each other, the becoming-one-person of man and wife before God, is a meaning of fulfillment of marriage in itself.

It is serious about Monsieur Henri! I don't like the sound of his letter. Be sure to talk it over with François, otherwise misunderstandings may arise. In no case and under no condition accept an invitation from him!

Ingrid T.

B. . . . . , November 19

Dear François,

My husband is away on a trip and can't write to you at present. So I am writing you a letter today. I should like to talk to you as if I were your sister.

God has placed a great treasure in your hands: Cecile's love. I would like to help you guard this treasure in the right way.

Love is not something which you can own, something which you can put in your pocket. Love is something you must win anew—over and over again. During the time of our engagement, Walter once wrote these lines to me:

"He who loves is no more alone. For the one whom he loves is always present. The one who loves has no wish to remain the center of his own life. He permits someone else to enter into the midst of it, and feels that is a great gain and happiness. He becomes empty like an open hand which holds nothing, but waits until something is put into it. He who loves has the courage to become someone who needs something."

What Cecile needs above all else is the assurance that you need her. How can you give her this assurance? Only in this way—that you tell her over and over again, "I love you. I need you." She can't hear it often enough. You must have the courage to "become someone who needs something."

A girl becomes afraid if a young man simply takes her love for granted and never bothers even to tell her that he loves her. Woman's love is different from mother love or sister love. Cecile's love can only blossom out to the fullest if it can be in answer to your own love.

Apostle Paul wrote to the church in Ephesus: "Husbands, love your wives, as Christ loved the Church." We love Christ because He has first loved us. Our love is an echo of His overwhelming love. It is strange that Paul never admonished the women to love their husbands . . .

I am not thinking now about physical love. You will never convince Cecile of your love by your caresses, your embraces and kisses alone. She wants to feel that your heart is seeking her heart and that you mean her herself and not just the beauty of her body.

A young man *is* his body. Your body, that's you. A girl feels herself *in* her body. Cecile senses that her inner being is not revealed just in her outward beauty. She wants to be loved for her own sake and not just for the sake of her beauty.

That's why your caresses are much less important to Cecile than is your whole way of acting. If you are polite to her, help her to get on her bicycle, open a door for her and let her go ahead of you—all that can mean more to her than a kiss. A woman who has been married for many years told me once with a sigh, "If only my husband would say 'Thank you' just once, when I have prepared an especially good meal."

Above all, it hurts a girl if you are more polite to others than you are to her. Then she notices that you treat her as if she were a piece of property.

When we met recently after church, you were very polite to me. You introduced me to Cecile, it's true. But during our whole conversation you didn't give her a chance to say a word. I had brought her a parcel of books which she could read as a preparation for marriage. As you went away, you let her carry the parcel . . .

You laugh. You laugh? That's such a little thing, you say, very unimportant. For a girl's heart, it is a big thing. For Cecile it is a very important thing.

Don't be stingy with words. Give her courage so that she can tell you what bothers her, what she misses in you. Listen to her lovingly, not just patiently. The most important thing is not that you are happy, but that you make her happy; not that you are understood, but that you understand . . .

Ingrid T.

Y. . . . . , November 30

Dear Madame Ingrid,

. . . Your letter comforted me most when you wrote and said that you also have troubles, anxieties and doubts. The white people always try to give us the impression that their married lives are ideal and without problems. Then we read in the papers about the many divorces in Europe and America—and we can't understand how the two go together.

That's why your letter meant all the more to me. I feel that I can tell you everything. By the way, the letter to my father is almost finished. On many slips of paper. All the thoughts that I would like to say to him if only I could. But I can't. I just can't force myself to send the letter.

Monsieur Henri gives me no peace. Here is another of his letters. Almost every day I get such a letter with all those insignificant phrases. They sound as if he had copied them out of a cheap love novel.

Thanks for your clear advice. I have refused the invitation through my friend Bertha. I'd rather not write to him myself. I do not wish a letter from me to him even to exist.

Cecile

Y. . . . . , November 19

Dear Mademoiselle Cecile,

I am very sorry that you have no time for me. But my love for you grows day to day. You are the crown of my heart. You are as beautiful as the moonlight.

I've already sent my brother to your father in K. He is in accord. I will send your father 50,000 francs soon. Then nothing will stand in the way of our happiness.

Next week there will be a big banquet for the high government officials. I would like to invite you to it. Your uncle will also attend.

You will be happy in our marriage. You can have servants and even earn money yourself. You can live like a white person. Our social life will only be in educated circles.

But love is most beautiful during the night . . .

Monsieur Henri

Y. . . . . , December 15

Dear Madame,

Two weeks of torture lie behind me. I've been waiting every day for a letter from you. But I know that you are alone with the children and that you have very little time before Christmas.

Monsieur Henri comes every day with his car to the school entrance. He follows us if we go out on our bicycles. He spies on us—where we go and what we do.

Recently I met him at my uncle's as I came home from school. Bertha's uncle was there too, the one who helped François to get his job. That's how I knew that everything was planned. Then we went to a cocktail party. Under this name the foreign embassies of the whole world introduce the so-called "civilization" to our society. My uncle, with whom I live, went too. We African girls can't refuse if our fathers command us to do something.

I didn't dance. But I couldn't avoid Monsieur Henri taking me home alone in his car. He said that he had decided to marry me. He said it just in that way. As if it would be a great favor on his part. He didn't even ask me what I thought about it.

He wanted to kiss me right away—just as one would bite into a banana. His breath smelled strongly of beer and liquor. It was repulsive.

He is twenty years older than I am, and he already has a wife and two children. He says she's uneducated, doesn't know French and refuses to live in the city. But since he has a position in the government he needs a wife in Y. whom he can present, who can receive guests and entertain them. That's why he chose me.

He made it clear that he can pay the bride-price for me.

His salary must be at least twenty times as much as François earns. He will visit my father and take with him all sorts of liquor and several cases of beer. He's already bought a radio for him and a sewing machine for my mother. He asked me what my brothers would like to have as gifts. I didn't answer him. I was glad that I could get out of the car without being molested. But I wept the whole night.

Money! A capital invested in women! The rich can buy them. The poor can at best rent a girl for a few nights, the kind of girl that nobody wants much anyway.

NO! I made a big mistake. Money doesn't give us value. It lowers us. It makes us just merchandise. It makes us either prostitutes or second and third wives of a rich man. That is no honorable African custom. That is no thank-offering to the parents. It is simply the slave trade.

If my father accepts money from Monsieur Henri I am lost. I shall be married to him. I shall just be Monsieur Henri's shop sign, his sign of business. Purpose of marriage: the wife is the salesman for the husband!

Of course, I've told François everything. If your husband wasn't away on a trip, he would have already written to him. François is again completely discouraged and has shrunk into himself, but I love him just that much more.

But what is the solution?

François thinks that if my father receives both money and gifts from Monsieur Henri, then there's only one thing for us to do—to run away.

What do you think about this solution? I need the answer quickly.

"He who believes doesn't flee . . ." That's right, but isn't it also flight if one is forced into a marriage and gives up the battle—gives up love . . . ?

Cecile

December 19

Dear Pastor and Madame,

This is the first letter addressed to both of you. We are writing it together.

We ran away. The answer to Cecile's letter of December 15 didn't reach us in Y. before we left. We think that probably you would have advised us not to run away. But we hope just the same that you will understand us. We couldn't see any other way out.

We had heard the news that Cecile's father had accepted 50,000 francs from Monsieur Henri. You know what that means. From now on he has a legal right to Cecile. To run away was our only weapon.

We decided together to do it, and we want to bear all the consequences together—even the bad ones. The fact that the school vacation has just begun made it easier for us to prepare everything without arousing suspicion.

You wrote to us once that the wedding day would be the day on which the marriage is born. You wrote: "A premature birth is dangerous."

But aren't there also births which are past due? Aren't they even more dangerous? And then the doctor has to intervene and sometimes he even has to do a Cesarean section. He has to cut the child out of the mother's womb in order to save its life.

Our running away is like a Cesarean section.

We don't know what is going to happen—where we shall live, or what we shall live on.

We only know one thing: now we are man and wife.

We have left father and mother. We cleave to one another. We have become one flesh. Genesis 2:24 is fulfilled. For that we need no money, no civil wedding, no pastor.

We need no tradition, no customs, no state and no church. We need no liquor, no paper and no singing.

We need only God. He will not forsake us. All others have forsaken us.

Our bride-price custom is no safeguard for marriage. It crushes marriage under its feet. It makes it possible to steal the bride by signing a check. Even the state supports the unmarried mother and the fatherless child. Those who want to marry must go empty handed. The Church advises us to wait, but it doesn't help us when we do that. It does not help us either, if we flee. No pastor would dare to receive us in his home.

You also haven't answered our last letters. We do not reproach you. We only ask that you do not reproach us, nor judge us. We would like to remain your children in the future.

Cecile is sick and lies in bed. She caught a bad cold the night we ran away. We had to go a long distance on foot. She sends special greetings to your children.

We are telling no one where we are, not even you. That is why you won't be able to write to us now. You can do only one thing—pray for us.

We believe that you will do this.

François and Cecile

To the Reader

During the course of our lives, God leads us again and again to borderlines where we must stand powerless and perplexed. For François and Cecile this borderline was called bride-price. For you and me it may have a different name. It may be called social status, racial prejudice, religious differences. Men or circumstances may cause it. The name of the borderline is not important. What counts is what we do when we come to it.

Did François and Cecile stand the test when they came to their borderline?

I must admit that I was disappointed when I returned from my trip and found the letter you have just read. I wished they would have had more patience. But with circumstances as they were, they had no other choice. In a way, their flight was a courageous step. Was there any other way for Cecile to escape marriage with Monsieur Henri? Surely marriage with him was not the will of God.

You ask why the fled into the wilderness. Why was there no one to receive and protect them? I'm afraid François is right: In Africa, it's hard to be a non-conformist. Nobody would risk a fight with the whole clan, just for the sake of two individuals. They evidently did not want me to become involved in such a fight either. To run away, as they did, is not rare in present-day Africa. Many couples are forced to choose this way, but with a more or less bad conscience.

Between the lines of their letter we can sense a faint trembling. And then as if to drown out an inner voice, they use a tone of mockery, which otherwise is foreign to them. Perhaps they feel already that they have made a mistake in thinking that through the physical union they become one flesh in the full sense of the word. Just as the baby must appear in the light of the world when it is born, so the legal act in public is essential to the consummation of marriage. Deep down in their hearts, when writing that letter, François and Cecile knew that they were guilty.

By their guilt, however, God opened my eyes to see my own. Suddenly I realized how much I had failed. I had not fought hard enough and not asked enough for divine guidance. Why hadn't I taken my trip at some other time? Why hadn't I gone to see Cecile or taken the trouble to visit her father in order to talk to him personally?

My wife wonders too how it was possible that she didn't answer Cecile's letter right away. Instead of taking François and Cecile by the hand and walking with them, my wife and I both feel as if we had only sent them radio messages from an airplane.

When we stand at the borderline ourselves we realize our own guilt. It then becomes crystal clear that we cannot exist without the reality of the cross of Jesus Christ. We can try to go around it by excusing ourselves and accusing others.

But if we face the Cross as those who are unable to live without forgiveness, then the experience of such a borderline becomes an encounter with God. Maybe the only way we can prove ourselves is to humbly accept our defeat. Those who face God become those who are faced by Him and the road continues even though in a different way than we think.

That was the case too with François and Cecile. Their

way led through deep valleys. The cold Cecile had caught during the flight developed into a serious pneumonia. Perhaps the inner conflict also weakened her outward resistance. In grave condition, she was taken at her own request to her home village.

François came and got me and I spent a week at her bedside which I shall not forget. For days we didn't know whether she could survive or not. Both she and François looked upon the sickness as a punishment and accepted it as such. When, almost miraculously, Cecile recovered we learned in a new way that all of us live by grace alone.

Cecile's father was deeply touched by all that happened. The possibility of losing his daughter suddenly by death changed all standards for him. Above all the letter which I want to share now at the end had an effect upon him. It points toward the future, not only for Cecile and François, but for all those who are in a similar situation.

It's the famous letter which we've already mentioned often, that Cecile wrote to her father. Not until she was desperately ill did François find the bits of paper upon which Cecile had made a rough copy of this letter. These were thoughts she had jotted down—often incomplete sentences. Much of what she had written was corrected, crossed out, then written anew and discarded once more. It was a moving testimony to the pains that the letter cost Cecile, to the struggle of a daughter's heart, to gain the love and understanding of her father.

I then put it all together, as one puts together the parts of a mosaic, copied it and sent it on to Cecile's father. There are signs that it was not written in vain.

Here is the letter:

Dear Father,

I have never written a letter to you before. It's very hard for me. But it would be even harder for me to talk to you. That's why I ask you to read these lines as if I were talking to you.

I will try to explain to you why I love François.

The picture I like best of him is the one in which he stretches out his hand. I can trust this hand. When I look at the picture, I always see him walking a little ahead of me. But then he stands still, turns around and gives me his hand to help me over the hard places. Then I come very near to him and he comforts me.

He can comfort me so wonderfully because I can answer him when he talks to me. I can take hold of his hand, because I'm not afraid when he stretches it out to me. He doesn't take advantage of his strength to make me feel inferior. And yet when I need protection, I'm sure that he is stronger than I am. I'm happy to be weak in his presence, because he doesn't make fun of me.

But he needs me too, and he's not ashamed to tell me. Even though he's strong and manly, he can also be helpless like a child. His strong hand then becomes an open, empty hand. It is then my greatest happiness to fill it.

That's what I mean when I say: I love François.

I know that you think I am a half-white when I write such things to you. You blame me for despising our African customs, because I want to marry the man I love and not one who is able to pay for me.

But the custom of bride-price is not exclusively African. They had it in Europe too, even in Israel. Wherever men became Christians this custom disappeared. I do not write to you as a Europeanized African, but as a Christian African.

As a Christian I believe that God has created me. To

Him alone I owe my life. No earthly father has ever paid God anything for his daughter. Therefore no earthly father has a right to make money out of her.

As a Christian I believe that Jesus Christ has died for me. He has paid the only price that can be paid for me: His blood. Any other price is the price for a slave.

As a Christian I believe that the Holy Spirit guides me. But I cannot follow His guidance unless I can choose freely.

Because I have chosen François of my own accord, I shall be faithful to him. Do you really think that the bride-price could hinder a wife from running away from her husband?

I have a friend whose father received $1,500 for her when she was married. She said to herself, "If my body is worth that much, then I can make some profit out of it for myself." She began to give herself to other men in exchange for money. There you have it: If the bride-price is acceptable and decent, then why not prostitution?

Or do you think that François would treat me better, if he had paid something for me? If he would take better care of me for that reason then I do not want to marry him. Then I would be only a thing to him. But I am a human being.

It's not true that money makes a wife more obedient and a husband more faithful. In the best case, money is a chain which must hold together there where no love is. But you can break a chain. You can give back money or goods. Love that has chosen freely is an unbreakable bond.

Dear Papa, please don't think that we are ungrateful. We love you dearly. We know what sacrifices you have made for me, especially when you sent me to school. We know too about your financial difficulties. We don't want to leave you in the lurch.

All we ask is this: Give us a start without debts. Allow us to found our own home. Only then can we really help you—really show you how grateful we are.

François makes the suggestion that we take my three brothers into our home when they go to school in Y. Isn't that a greater proof of his love for me than if he gives you money which doesn't belong to him?

Dear Papa, give us a chance! Let us begin!